BEER

7,000 BC onwards (all flavours)

First published in October 2013
Reprinted September 2014 and October 2015

A catalogue record for this book is available from the British Library

ISBN 978 0 85733 130 4

Library of Congress control no. 2013941312

Published by Haynes Publishing,
Sparkford, Yeovil,
Somerset BA22 7JJ, UK.
Tel: 01963 442030 Fax: 01963 440001
Int. tel: +44 1963 442030 Int. fax: +44 1963 440001
E-mail: sales@haynes.co.uk
Website: www.haynes.co.uk

Haynes North America Inc.,
861 Lawrence Drive, Newbury Park,
California 91320, USA.

Printed in the USA by Odcombe Press LP,
1299 Bridgestone Parkway, La Vergne, TN 37086.

Acknowledgements

With thanks to the Home Brew Shop for letting us take pictures in their store and warehouse. Also special thanks to Cath Harries, not just for her original photography, but for access to her extensive picture library.

Front cover photograph: *Guy Harrop.*

BEER

7,000 BC onwards (all flavours)

Enthusiasts' Manual

The practical guide to the history, appreciation and brewing of beer

Tim Hampson

Everybody needs something to believe in.

I believe I will have another beer!

If they don't serve beer in heaven then I'm not going.

Contents

INTRODUCTION
BREWING
GREAT BEER

Brewers Association

Beer Genie

▼ **Home brewing offers a doorway through into a new world of taste, flavour and imagination.**

(Cath Harries)

Warning! This book could change your life...

Most books about home brewing tell readers how to make beers at home that are not only the same as they drink in a pub, but are also cheaper. This book is much more than that. Not only does it describe beer from its earliest days up to the present time, but it's also intended to give the reader the skills to produce beers which will surpass commercial creations. And yes, they could be cheaper than beer from a pub, but that's not the point.

Becoming a home brewer is to become part of a growing movement which embraces both men and women, the younger streetwise and the older and more sedate. Some might secretly want to turn a hobby into a profession, others might be professionals piloting new beers at home, or enthusiasts brewing to entertain themselves and their friends.

In the United States home brewing is a seriously cool hobby for tens of thousands of people. Most towns have at least one home brewing club and there's an annual convention where thousands of different beers can be tasted. And the signs are that something similar could be happening in the UK.

It's never been easier to get into home brewing. The basic equipment and ingredients are readily available, and there can be few activities which provide such a rewarding outcome. Of course, not every home-brewed beer will be a world class creation, but with some experience, the correct procedures and some pretty simple equipment the beers you make will often be better brews than can be bought from a supermarket or local pub. And it doesn't matter what kind of beer you like – ale, stout, fruit beers or winter warmers – not only can you make it at home, you can make it well.

Getting brewing

It's all in the name. Home brewing is the hobby of brewing beer at home. It's easy, fun and very rewarding, and you end up with the beer to drink.

Anyone can do it. You don't need lots of equipment to make quality beer. If you can open a can of soup and heat it, then you can make beer.

It's not going to cost you lots either. A basic kit, with everything you need, can easily be found for around £30–£40. Some are even cheaper.

Will I have the time?

Well, from start to finish, and depending on the beer, it will take about three to four weeks to make your first beer:

- Brewing – two hours.
- Fermentation – ten days.
- Bottling – one hour; a cask would be even quicker.
- Conditioning – two weeks.
- Time to drink a glass – that depends on your thirst...

Brewing at home is a tactile, aural experience, and it's also fun. It's a journey in pursuit of excellence and perfection, but don't be downhearted when things don't always go to plan. If you learn from these experiences they'll make you a better brewer.

Home brewing offers people the opportunity to be creative, and through the use of their craftsmanship and efforts to participate in something that's part of a cultural heritage which goes back to ancient times. There's something elemental about creating a brew that's shared by people not just for the enjoyment of the beer, but because it brings them together to talk, laugh and reflect on the good things in life.

KEEP CALM AND MAKE HOMEBREW BEER

The home brewer will become the maestro, conducting an orchestra of natural ingredients. Beer is usually made from four simple notes – malt, hops, yeast and water – from which can be produced a seemingly limitless symphony of colours, tastes and aromas. And the home brewer's creativity doesn't stop with that. The beer will need a name, and a label might need to be designed for the bottles or the barrel.

And as the home brewer gets more confident, so begins their journey into a world of unusual ingredients and the pursuit of new tastes. Perhaps you'll experiment with some herbs and spices off the kitchen shelf, or cherries foraged from a neighbour's garden. Once the basics of brewing have been mastered the only limitation is the imagination of the brewer.

But home brewing is also about history. Keen brewers soon start to delve into the past to discover what the beers were like that were drunk by people in medieval England or 19th-century Germany. Beer culture embraces thousands of years of human history and scores of different styles, with each having its own flavour. Then there's the pleasure of matching beer with food and discovering that beer is often a better partner to many dishes than wine can ever be.

Creating your maiden home brew is the first step on a journey that will bring you new friends and take you to different places. Beer is a social lubricant that fires people's imagination and conversation. Brewers, be they humble creators of beer at home or those who work for commercial producers, love to talk and swap ideas and recipes.

The time for beer has come.

Beer Genie

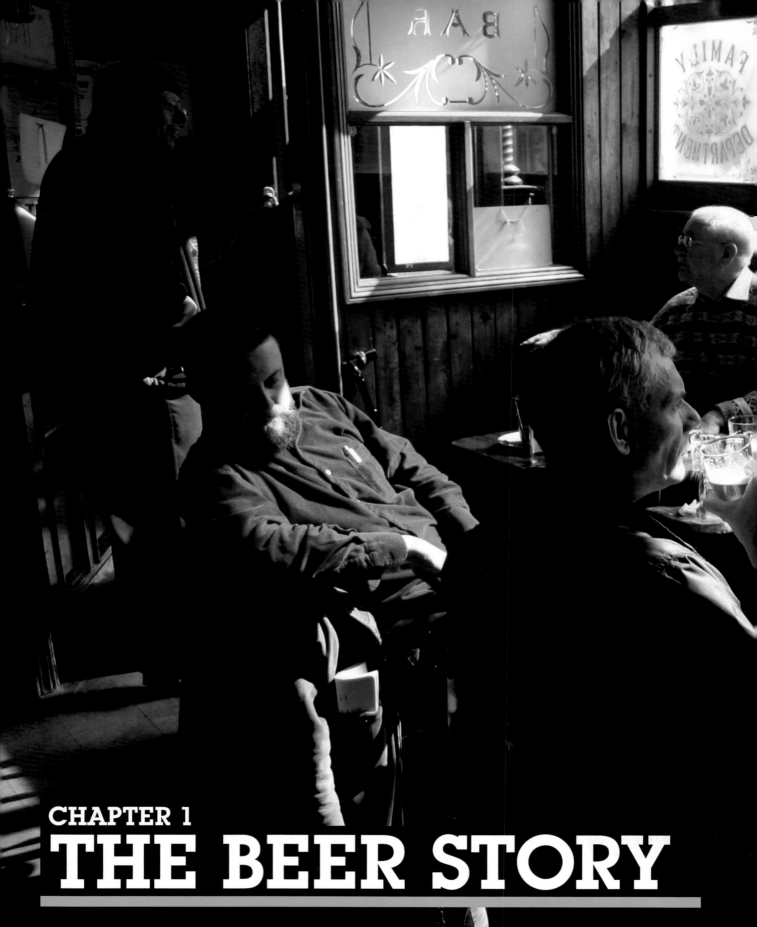

CHAPTER 1
THE BEER STORY

Tim Hampson

The origins and history of beer

So was beer first brewed in China? The truth is that we don't know, but it seems that some 9,000 years ago, either in China or in the sweeping crescent-shaped fertile plains of Mesopotamia, which is now in Syria, nomadic hunter gatherers started to grow and harvest an ancient form of grain and set up settlements near their pastures.

▲ In ancient times, as now, the drinking of beer was one of life's simple pleasures.

◄ In ancient Egypt, beer was the drink of the people and it was made every day. (Getty Images)

Archaeological evidence shows that this grain could have been used to make an early form of beer. Humans were on the long path to civilisation. Whether beer is solely responsible for our civilisation is debatable, but it was important. An ancient oral poem from Babylonia called *The Gilgamesh Epic* tells the story of the civilising influence of drinking beer. It relates the story of Enkidu, a shaggy, unkempt beast of a man, who after spending a week with a woman was taught to eat bread and drink beer. After that he washed and became civilised.

By the time of the Ancient Egyptians drinking beer had been firmly established as one of life's simple but essential pleasures. An intoxicating drink made from grain was used to honour the dead, and Osiris – the green-skinned god of the afterlife – was the patron deity of brewers. Wine in Ancient Egypt was a drink of the elite, but beer was the drink of the people. In the tombs of pharaohs wine was given as an offering to the gods, while beer was also placed there as a provision for their servants' journey to the next life. Also, every household was equipped with simple brewing equipment. Beer was a staple of everyday life – in effect a liquid form of bread.

Throughout Africa there are examples of beers made from millet or sorghum, one of the oldest grains still used for beer making. Professor Patrick McGovern, of the University of

Pennsylvania Museum of Archaeology and Anthropology, has studied a 3,000-year-old millet drink, which was preserved inside a tightly lidded bronze vessel from a tomb in the Shang Dynasty capital of Anyang in the fertile earth of the Yellow River valley in China.

McGovern says he has found evidence showing that early people were making similar alcoholic drinks as far back as 7000 BC, his examination of pottery chips found in a Neolithic village of that date at Jiahu in China revealing that they include traces of the chemical compounds found in alcoholic drinks.

The remains from China, along with a pattern of ancient brews found in other regions of the world such as Africa and South and Central America, has led McGovern to conjecture that alcohol had a pivotal role in the development of early man. Why make bread when beer will do?

One of the oldest forms of beer still produced today is sake. The Japanese drink is known as a rice wine, but it's technically a beer, as it's a fermented grain. According to tradition it was a drink of the Imperial Palace, and was imbibed to bring people closer to the gods. However, it's likely that it

was first produced for domestic consumption before it was elevated to a higher plane.

The production of sake involves first polishing the rice. Next the whole village would have chewed the rice and nuts and spat the mixture into a big tub. The sake produced was *kuchikami no sake*, which means 'chewing the mouth sake'. The chewing released enzymes in the grain necessary for fermentation.

A similar technique was used in Central and South America to make a drink called *chicha* – made with maize, peppercorns and local fruit, which would help kick-start the fermentation process. Some of the maize was ground, chewed, mixed with saliva and then spat out and made into small cakes, which were flattened and dried in the sun. Enzymes in the saliva break down the starch in the maize to release the sugars necessary for fermentation. Also the chewing would have helped sterilise the sugars in the cake, stopping them being spoiled by wild yeasts and bacteria.

In 2009 the American brewery Dogfish Head made its own version of *chicha*. Brewer Sam Caligone said it took six people all day to chew through 3kg of Peruvian blue corn. The following year he and his workers chewed their way through 15kg of grain. All that chewing must have been thirsty work.

So where was beer brewed first? In truth we'll probably

▼ **In modern Africa the ancient grain sorghum is still used to make beer.** (SABMiller)

◀ **Brewing, like the discovery of fire, probably began in different parts of the world at around the same time.** (Getty Images)

never know, but it seems fair to assume that brewing, like the use of fire, could have developed almost simultaneously in different parts of the world.

The early brews from South America could provide a clue to one of the beer world's greatest mysteries: where did lager yeast – which ferments at a lower temperature than ale yeast – come from? Well, scientists reckon they've finally found the answer to that question.

In Europe, brewing gradually evolved during the Middle Ages to produce ale-type beer, a process that uses *Saccharomyces cerevisiae*, the same species involved in producing wine and leavened bread. According to a study in *Proceedings of the National Academies of Sciences*, lager beer was first brewed in Europe in the 15th century. This employs an allotetraploidhybrid yeast, *Saccharomyces pastorianus*, a domesticated species created by the fusion of a *Saccharomyces cerevisiae* ale yeast with an unknown cryotolerant Saccharomyces species.

Well, after a five-year search the scientists say they've discovered, identified and named the organism, a species of wild yeast called *Saccharomyces eubayanus* that lives on orange-coloured galls on beech trees in the Patagonian region of Argentina. Which is a long, long way from Bavaria, the spiritual home of lager brewing. Apparently, Patagonian natives used to make a fermented drink from the galls, which was the clue that told scientists they might have found the missing microbiological link. But how the yeast found its way 8,000 miles across the Atlantic must remain conjecture. Perhaps it came back with Christopher Columbus when he returned from his transatlantic voyage to the New World in 1492. Or it could have come to Europe earlier, with Vikings returning from their own voyages to the far side of the world. We just don't know.

In Cyprus, researchers at the Early-Middle Bronze Age settlement of Kissonerga-Skalia, near Paphos, led by Dr Lindy Crewe from the University of Manchester, have excavated a two-metre by two-metre mud-plaster domed structure, which they say was used as a kiln to dry malt and make beer 3,500 years ago.

Beers of different flavours would have been brewed from malted barley and fermented with yeasts with an alcoholic content of around 5% – the yeast would have been either wild or produced from fruit such as grapes or figs. According to the archaeologists beer was commonly drunk because it was more nutritious than bread and was less likely to contain harmful pathogens than the available water, which could make people ill.

Alcoholic beverages were also used to oil the wheels of business and pleasure in much the same way as today. Work brought communities together for tasks such as bringing in the harvest or erecting special buildings.

Archaeologists Billy Quinn and Declan Moore say that one of the most common archaeological monuments still found in the Irish landscape could have been used for brewing. These are the enigmatic *fulacht fiadh*, of which more than 4,500 survive, dating back 4,000 years or so. They're small, horseshoe-shaped, grass-covered mounds, conventionally described by archaeologists as ancient cooking spots. However, Quinn and Moore believe that they could have been used as breweries. According to Quinn: 'The tradition of brewing in Ireland has a long history, we think that the *fulacht* may have been used as a kitchen sink, for cooking, dyeing, many uses, but that a primary use was the brewing of ale. It became clear to us that the making of beer was one of the first steps in turning man into civilised man and that beer making came before bread making.'

To prove their theory, Quinn and Moore set out to recreate the process. The experiment was carried out in the backyard of Billy Quinn's home in Cordarragh, Headford, Co Galway. 'Seeking authenticity in replicating our Bronze Age ale we decided that our equipment should be as basic as possible,' said Quinn. So they used an old wooden trough filled with water and added heated stones. After achieving an optimum temperature of 60–70°C they began to add milled barley, and after 45 minutes simply baled the final product into fermentation vessels. They added natural wild flavourings – wisely taking care to avoid anything toxic or hallucinogenic – and then added yeast from the Galway Brewery, after cooling the vessels in a bath of cold water for several hours. According to Moore, 'including the leftover liquid we could easily have produced up to 300 litres of this most basic ale'.

Through their experiments they discovered that the process of brewing ale in a *fulacht* using hot-rock technology is a simple process. To produce the ale took only a few hours, followed by a three-day wait to allow for fermentation.

Quinn and Moore point out that although their theory is based solely on circumstantial and experimental evidence, they believe that although probably multifunctional in nature, one use of the *fulacht fiadh* could certainly have been for brewing beer.

'Beer is liquid bread,' added Quinn, 'and if our theory is correct it is the making of beer that turned the savage beast into the civilised man.'

▲ **Irish archaeologists Billy Quinn (left) and Declan Moore brewed a Bronze Age-style ale in a homemade fulacht fiadh in Quinn's backyard.** (Quinn and Moore)

▼ **Quinn and Moore say a fulacht fiadh may have had many uses, including beer making, just like a kitchen sink.** (Quinn and Moore)

The first millennia

An exposed fort in what is now Northumbria, in the north-west of England, where the Romans were fighting a guerrilla war with the local Celtic tribes, plays an important part in the history of brewing in Britain.

In the 1980s, in a waterlogged rubbish tip left behind by the retreating Roman invaders, archaeologists discovered 400 slivers of sodden birch, alder and oak wood, known as the Vindolanda tablets. Created between AD 90–130, they bear written communications between officers at the fort and the outside world.

▼ **A modern brew house might look technologically advanced, but it wouldn't take a medieval brewer long to find out how everything worked.** (Tim Hampson)

One, from a cavalry officer named Masculus, tells his commander that 'My fellow soldiers have no beer. Please order some to be sent.' Then as now the morale of the troops was essential to the war effort, and what could be better than beer to keep the soldiers in good humour? On another is recorded the name of a brewer, one Atrectus, but alas that's all we know of the man. He probably ate a diet that included roe deer, olives, bacon, oysters, wheat, beer and honey, and if he was lucky he would have lived into his 40s; but his significance is that he's the first named brewer in British history.

Brewing had been taking place on these islands for hundreds if not thousands of years. The Celts were prolific brewers and are thought to have made a beer using heather. An example of such a beer is still brewed today, from a recipe which – its current brewers Scott and Bruce Williams claim – was first brewed by a Pictish king. The Williams brothers' first brewing venture was the Heather Ale Company, where they began to produce *fraoch*, which was brewed with sprigs of fresh heather picked from the Ochill Hills near their brewery. The recipe, written in Gaelic, had been given to Bruce when he was running a homebrew shop in Glasgow, by a woman whose goal was to try to recreate a recipe made famous by an old legend of a Pictish king who supposedly threw himself off a cliff after a Scots king attempted to coax the recipe from him by capturing and torturing his son. According to the story, the recipe was for *leanne fraoch*, or heather ale. The translated recipe was subsequently developed by then home-brewer Bruce into the recipe that's used today. The tawny beer has floral and peaty aromatic flavours, which come from the use of flowering heather instead of hops. Other botanicals picked from hedgerows and moorland are added to the brew, among them the catkins and leaves of sweet willow, also known as bog myrtle, which add even more soaring aromatics. Some ginger is also added, to give the brew a bittersweet piquancy.

The Celts made progress in understanding the process of allowing cereal to germinate, which we call malting. The Celts called the process *braces*, which is the stem of the French word brassiere.

By AD 500 the Angles and Saxons had started arriving in Britain. Much of their social life revolved around beer and alehouses, and it seems they developed the technology of building large hooped casks for carrying ale. These settlers seemed to recognise three main types of beer or ale: mild, which was fresh and probably quite sweet; clear, probably older and sourer; and Welsh, which was possibly made with wheat and honey – a brewing style already well known to the Welsh, who had been drinking bragget or honey beers for centuries. Such beers didn't use hops and it's likely that they had to be drunk within days of being made, as they could soon go off.

Ale, along with bread, had become recognised as a normal and essential part of daily life, and by the 9th century roadside alehouses had become commonplace, with the ale brewed on the premises. These buildings were identified by long poles, to which a leafy branch was attached if they sold wine. The era of the pub sign had begun.

The church too had started to play an important role in people's lives. The large religious establishments set aside rooms for travellers and visitors, many of whom would be travelling to visit shrines and important places of worship. Beer produced in the monastery's own brewery would have

▲ **Across medieval Europe the brewing of beer became commonplace and well organised.**

been served to the weary travellers. Often the priests would point out to travellers who had perhaps had a beer too many that it was not sinful to drink beer, but it was abuse that was the problem. Society, as we know it, was developing.

Across temperate Europe brewing was also on the increase. By AD 770 Emperor Charlemagne the Great was appointing brewers, and brewing was already taking place in what were to become some of the world's great brewing locations, in Pilsen in Bohemia, Bavaria in Germany, Leuven in Belgium and Burton upon Trent in England. Within decades of the start of the 2nd century brewing was also under way at two monasteries in Germany, Weltenburger Klosterbrauereir and Weihenstephan, both of which today claim to be the oldest site for continuous brewing in the world.

Outside of the monasteries, most brewing in Europe was done by women, who were known as brewsters. Indeed, women would be the principle brewers of beer for centuries, until industrialisation of the brewing process saw the role pass to men. However, today both men and women brew beer, whether at home or commercially.

The Industrial Revolution

Agriculturist and writer William Ellis, who began employment as a customs officer and then worked in the brewing industry in London, was quite a man. He wrote *The London and Country Brewer*, a groundbreaking publication in the literature of technical brewing, and we should rise a glass of beer in celebration of his life.

First published in 1734, eight editions of *The London and Country Brewer* were produced between then and 1759. It is one of the most important beer books ever written, as it describes for the first time the application of scientific processes to practices that had previously been solely empirical. It explains the many aspects of the brewing process, such as malting and mashing, in technical detail, and in its later editions describes how to make clear beer. Through its description we can gauge the scale and size of the brewing industry at that time, and its reliance on the new era of industrial technology.

Ellis says that the book was written for the many inhabitants of cities and towns, as well as travellers, who have for a long time suffered 'great prejudices' from unwholesome and unpleasant beers and ales.

For the first time the production of pale, amber and brown malts is described, including the effect of different types of kiln, fuel and temperature.

◀ **Hogarth's famous print** *Beer Street*, **published in 1751, shows the many benefits of moderate consumption.**

▼ **The Industrial Revolution slowly brought an end to country-house and farm-kitchen brewing.** (Tim Hampson)

▶ **A cooper's skills were essential to make the vessels needed to brew and store beer.** (Tim Hampson).

It was at this time that James Watt improved the steam engine, and brewers began to use such engines to pump water and grind malt. In addition Britain's growing canal network enabled raw materials and the beer itself to be transported many miles. Slowly the brewing industry began to coalesce into bigger units, many of which are still known today, including Bass, Whitbread, Worthington, Courage and Tetley.

As the population increased to more than nine million, so brewers had to move out of their farmhouses and kitchens to enable the brewing trade to respond by massively increasing production. The age of industry had arrived, and with it an era of scientific advancement, which saw thermometers and hydrometers/ saccharometers added to the brewer's repertoire of equipment. The saccharometer enabled brewers to measure the amount of fermentable sugar material available, the wort, and to use the malt in a more efficient way, while the thermometer stopped brewers needing to plunge a finger into boiling liquid in an effort to gauge its temperature. Up till then, boiling wort was only recognised as being too hot when clumps of malt formed in it. While the art and craft of brewing was thus augmented by science,. mechanisation moved into the brewery – valves, pumps, and cast iron and copper vessels were now found in breweries as they grew bigger.

The work of chemist Louis Pasteur – who managed to show that beer could be brewed under hygienic, sterile conditions – had a profound effect on the quality of beer which people drank. However, it was developments in refrigeration that perhaps had the biggest effect on brewing, which ultimately led to temperature control of the brewing process. Without temperature control there couldn't be large modern breweries, nor could lager-style beers be produced on such a large scale worldwide. Refrigeration is used in two main areas in the brewery: to cool the wort and to keep it at a low temperature for long periods of time while the beer matures. The work of the brewer was no longer orchestrated by the ambient temperature of the air. The brewer had the control of his environment.

▲ **The rich story of beer through the ages is charted at the National Brewing Centre, Burton upon Trent.** (National Brewing Centre)

▼ **The Burton Union fermentation system, one of the marvels of the Industrial Revolution, can still be seen at Marston's brewery in Burton upon Trent.**
(Tim Hampson)

With scientific advancement came development in the design of breweries and the positioning of the brewing vessels. One of England's greatest brewers is Marston's in Burton upon Trent, which still uses a fermentation system called the Burton Union developed at this time. In the 1860s brewers from around the world travelled to this brewing Mecca to see this new technology in operation. Indeed, stepping inside the Victorian fermentation room with its high vaulted ceiling is to enter one of the world's great brewing temples. Here can be seen the lines of interlinked wooden barrels and fermenters which give Marston's its greatest brew, its Pedigree.

Like the pipes of a glorious cathedral organ, supported by a double-deck scaffold of iron, snaking pipes take the fermenting beer from large oak barrels at the bottom up into a trough above. It's the vibrant movement of the fermenting wort passing from the barrel to the trough and back again that helps create the complexity of the Pedigree. As it dances through the union it adds strength and intensity to its taste.

Gravity too became the brewers' friend, with many of the most modern of the Victorian breweries being built in a tower formation. The brewing process begins at the top of the tower and the power of gravity moves the ingredients down through the brewing process to where the casks are filled in the basement.

One of the remaining Victorian tower breweries can still be seen today in the village of Hook Norton in North Oxfordshire. Brewing began on this site more than 160 years ago, and the 'new' brewery, which was completed in 1899, is a near perfect example of a tower brewery. William Bradford, the doyen of the era's brewery architects, designed it. Harvey's Bridge Wharf brewery in Lewes in Sussex is another survivor which is still hard at work. Both breweries share the architect's signature decorative elements based on a Queen Anne revival style, including ironwork, an ornate roofline and fenestration.

The Hook Norton brewery still has its original steam engine, installed in 1895, in working order. Though now rarely used it's often fired up on the brewery's open days, when the public can appreciate that the making of Hook Norton's beers remains a tactile, aural and visual experience, where tradition, craft, science and technology are brought together.

▲ The Hook Norton brewery, in the Oxfordshire village of the same name, looks much the same as when it was first built more than 100 years ago. (Tim Hampson)

▼ A farrier has to replace the shoes of working horses on a regular basis. (Hook Norton)

▲ The village of Hook Norton often sounds to the 'clip-clop' of horses' hooves as the dray delivers beer to local pubs. (Tim Hampson)

▼ Harvey's, in Lewes, Sussex, might be old, but it's no museum, as it is still a vibrant working brewery. (Cath Harries)

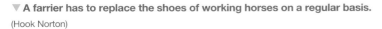

Modern brewing in the UK

Something of a beer revolution is currently taking place in the UK. While the sales of beer from the big national and international brewers have stalled, a microbrewing revolution is taking place. In the last few years hundreds of home brewers who'd dreamt of turning their hobby into a business have gone out and done just that.

One such enthusiast is 30-year home brewing veteran Ed Murray, who finally tired of driving around the country as a management consultant. Now he commutes a mere 700m from one side of the Oxfordshire village of Horspath, where he lives, to his brewery, Shotover Brewing Co. Indeed, beer not blood must run in his veins, as his father was a keen home brewer before him, and one of his sons kick-started this venture when he wrote a school project on how to set up a brewery. (His son's conclusion was not to do it!)

Ed's approach to brewing is uncompromising, as he wants to produce beers with an attractive and complex flavour profile by combining the highest quality ingredients, skill and patience. And like many of the new wave of commercial brewers, his eyes aren't set on world domination, with hundreds of miles between the drinker and the brewery: he wants to produce beers for local people. 'We're an Oxford brewery and our market is Oxfordshire,' says Ed.

▼ The Kelham Island Tavern in Sheffield is famed for its range of beers from small, independent breweries. (Tim Hampson)

He describes himself as a craft brewer. The beer is hand-made in batches of 1,200 litres from floor-malted barley, malted wheat and hops, then hand casked and hand bottled. 'We don't pasteurise or chill filter or artificially carbonate our beer,' he says. 'It's a fresh product naturally conditioned by secondary fermentation in the cask or bottle.'

Also typical of the new wave of brewers while he has one eye on tradition and the need to respect it, he's not afraid to experiment. When creating his India Pale Ale, for instance, he added handfuls of Oxfordshire-grown Fuggles hops for bitterness and aroma. He also added, as do many of the new wave of brewers, 'big flavour' hops from New Zealand's South Island and the North-West Pacific coast of the USA.

Another Oxfordshire brewer starting to create new and exciting beers, using different ingredients and processes, is Mattias Sjöberg, founder of the Compass Brewery. Raised in a small town just south of Stockholm, Mattias started home brewing when he was 16 years old. He quickly became fascinated with the chemistry and biology of beer, and this led him to apply to a degree course in Brewing and Distilling at Herriot-Watt University in Scotland.

Mattias says that beer needs to reclaim its rightful position on the dinner table as a complement to any food. He brews his beers for flavour rather than to strictly adhere to a style. One of his beers is called Symposium, which he says has cooled the fire of Caribbean ginger beer by brewing it like a Bavarian wheat beer. The cloudy beer's clove and lemon flavours mingle with spicy ginger to create a thirst-quenching tipple, which partners well with salmon or gravlax. It can also serve as a complement to dishes where ginger, lemon grass, coriander and cloves are present.

His Christmas special, Tannenbaum, draws on German influences. It's dark, strong and complex. The aroma hops

▲ **Large or small, old or new – good science and record keeping are essential for the brewing of great beer.** (Cath Harries)

have been chosen for spice notes, balanced with the herbal character of Oxfordshire spruce needles. Added to British malt is a touch of German sour malt, for a tangy note.

The popularity of microbreweries is part of a general increase of interest in food and drink being shown by British consumers. Research by the Campaign for Real Ale finds there are now more than 1,000 breweries operational across the UK, the highest number for over 70 years. Such an astonishing number is put into context when one realises that the actual total of 1,009 is five times more breweries than were operational 30 years ago, four times more than there were 20 years ago, and more than twice as many as there were a decade ago.

A double-dip recession has done nothing to halt the incredible surge in the number of brewers coming on stream, making the small brewing sector surely one of the most remarkable UK industry success stories of the last decade. In fact, the boom in new breweries has, in many cases, made the term 'micro' obsolete, with some small brewers having become remarkably large, installing new equipment or doubling production to keep up with demand.

But the British brewing industry, like Janus, can look backwards as well as forwards. There's a trade association called the Independent Family Brewers of Britain. Its membership now only numbers about 30 companies, but they share several things in common – a heritage which is likely to go back at least 100 years and continuing involvement with the families who helped to establish them.

One such is the Hook Norton brewery in Oxfordshire, which we've already mentioned. Its head brewer James Clarke is the great-great-grandson of the founder of the brewery, John

▲ **Cleanliness is next to godliness in a modern brew house like Adnams.** (Tim Hampson)

◀ **Stainless steel has replace copper in most contemporary breweries.** (Tim Hampson)

Harris, who started brewing on the site in 1856. But though the brewery has a long and illustrious history, it doesn't live in the past. As James Clarke says, 'We were a modern brewery when we first opened,' and his ambition is that while preserving the provenance and integrity of the brewery and the beers, it will remain a modern company. 'My great-great-grandfather would have used stainless steel if it had been available,' he says.

The success of brewers, young or old, big or small, means that today's beer drinkers have an enormous and greater variety of choice than ever seen before. This is because, whilst historically there were more breweries in the pre-1930s period, modern distribution and communication networks mean that the wide variety of beers available has never been so accessible to consumers or to pubs wanting to serve locally produced beer. As a rough rule of thumb, there's now one brewery for every 50 pubs in the UK. And that's something we should all say cheers to.

Europe's beer heritage

Travel Europe or even the world and walk into any bar in a posh hotel, airport lounge or holiday resort and you'd be forgiven for thinking that beer was only brewed by four or five companies.

Despite the richness of brewing heritage which sees many countries having their own distinct beer culture, which is usually defined by custom and legislation, most people seem to be drinking a style of brew that's yellow in colour, served at about 5°C, and is loosely based on a Pilsner recipe and barely has the merest hint of any hop character. But this apparent blandness is a cloak to the rich tapestry of beer culture that stretches from stout drinkers in Ireland to people sipping on glasses of Imperial stout in St Petersburg.

A superficial view of European alcohol consumption would define the British as drinking warm beer by the pint in pubs, the Germans as clashing steins of lager while munching on bratwurst, and the majority of French as preferring to drink glasses of wine. But the world of beer is much more diverse and dynamic than that, and redolent with bibulous extravaganza. Here are some of the stories.

The Czech Republic is regarded by some as the greatest brewing nation in the world. Its place in beer's pantheon of greats is assured, as it's home to the town of Plzen, whose burghers commissioned Bavarian Josef Grolle to develop a new beer for the Plzensky Prazdroj Brewery which could rival a new style being brewed in Vienna. At the time, the locally

produced beer was probably top-fermented and expensive to buy. Also, up to this point many beers from the area were brown in colour. Grolle's clear, golden, cold-fermented beer was a revelation. Pleasing to the eye when poured into the glassware, which had only recently become widely available, its use of fragrant and spicy Zatec hops and sweet Moravian malt made it an instant success. Named 'Pilsner Urquell' – meaning 'from Plzen', the original source – its fame quickly spread far and wide. Since then the pilsen style has been copied and parodied but rarely emulated around the world, and the term is often used to describe most golden, lagered beers.

▼ **Staff and families celebrate 100 years of brewing at the Budweiser Bier Burgerbrau in 1895.** (Getty Images)

▲ **The town of Bamberg in Germany is home to a number of fine breweries.** (Tim Hampson)

Today, many new brewers are joining the Czech beer scene. On the outskirts of Pilsen in the Czech Republic is the Hotel Purkmistr, where a brewery opened in 2007. The brewery's range includes an unfiltered pale lager, a cherry beer and an interesting cappuccino-flavoured beer. The hotel's

▼ **After a tour of the Krombacher brewery, what could be better than a freshly poured glass of its beer?** (Tim Hampson)

bar is large, spacious and dominated by two copper kettles, which are overseen by brewer Petr Mic. He says: 'Euro-beer tastes all the same – I want to do something different.' Once a year, in September, the hotel hosts a beer festival which features more than 140 beers from the Republic's new wave of brewers, where drinkers can discover there's much more to Czech beer than just the glorious pilsen.

Germany once had more commercial breweries than any other country in the world, but the United States now takes that honour. However, German brewers still number more than 1,000, and although most brew Pilsner-style beers it remains much more than a one-beer nation, as more than 15 classic beer styles are brewed. Germany is a country with strong regional identities, which are exemplified by its many local food favourites, and likewise its local beers. Smoky-flavoured *rauchbier* is served in Bamberg; in Cologne drinkers can enjoy the delights of the softly-spoken and fresh *Kölsch*, served by blue-aproned *kobes*; and travellers to Berlin can seek out acidic *weissbier*, while *altbiers* can be sampled in towns along the Rhine.

Dortmund is renowned for its dark *altbiers*. One translation of *alt* might be 'old', and it's said these beers are so-called because they pre-date the 'newer' Pilsner. However, it's more likely that the word has a Latin root and it would be better translated as 'high', denoting that the beer is top-fermented, with a yeast head forming on top of the fermenting beer. A Düsseldorfer *alt* is served fresh and fast from a wooden cask. Brown in colour, with a large white foaming head, these beers have a refreshing bitter sweetness, but not as bitter as English

▲ **The beautiful medieval town of Bamberg, Germany, is a must-visit destination for any beer fan.** (Tim Hampson)

▲ **Brussels, in Belgium, is home to some of the world's greatest beer bars.** (Tim Hampson)

ale – they have the full maltiness one has come to expect from a German beer.

However, at heart most German brewers are deeply conservative and most produce a drinkable pilsen, a darker lager known as a *dunkel* and a low-hopped but highly carbonated *hefeweizen* or wheat beer.

The country is well known for its beer purity thanks to the *Reinheitsgebot* – a guiding set of principles devised in Bavaria in the 16th century which states that only barley malt, hops and water can be used to produce beer.

Belgium is a glorious paradise for the beer lover. From Flanders come sour red ales. The city of Brussels promises *gueuze*, *lambic* and *krieks*. Elsewhere can be found Wallonian *saisons*, *wit biers*, and monasteries which brew some of the best beers in the world. More than 25 indigenous beer styles have been identified in the country. Brussels probably has some of the best beer bars in the world, where beers will be carefully poured into dedicated glasses by attentive waiters.

Brussels is also home to the Cantillon Brewery, a working, brewing and living museum. Here the Van Roy family have been making their acetic *gueuze* beers – a blend of old and new *lambic* – for over 100 years. Wild yeast gave humans their first beers, but science has long since dictated that most beers aren't made in this way, simply left exposed to the air to await seeding by the living organism. But this remains exactly how *lambics* are produced, which come from the six

or so breweries along the Zenne valley where the technique of wild fermentation is still used to produce beers with almost manic winey, soaring fruit and smoky flavours. An ideal and surprising accompaniment to food, if most of the beers of the world are as smooth and as cultured as a Bach concerto

▼ **The Cantillon brewery in Brussels is a working museum and living brewery.** (Tim Hampson)

▲ The brewing equipment at the Cantillon brewery in Brussels might look ordinary, but the results are extraordinary. (Tim Hampson)

▶ Jean Van Roy delights in serving his distinctive beers at Cantillon, which was founded by his great, great, grandfather in 1900. (Tim Hampson)

▼ Cantillon is home to some remarkable wild yeasts, which give each brew a different vibrancy and character. (Tim Hampson)

▶ **Beer in Italy is appealing to a new, younger audience of drinkers.** (SABMiller)

then these wild brews are as challenging as one of Stockhausen's 'aletory' (controlled chance) compositions.

Italy, the land of the grape and the olive might seem a surprising entrant in a list of great brewing countries, but 'Brewed in Italy' is now a mark of creativity and quality. In the 1990s many former Italian home brewers moved into commercial production in small brewpubs, and drinkers discovered that they liked the taste of unfiltered and unpasteurised beers. Today the country has more than 180 small brewers and brewpubs and their numbers are rising. Former home brewer Agostino Arioli developed a passion for beer after visiting the Granville Island brewery in Vancouver, Canada. At Birrificio Italiano in Marione, on the way to the Swiss border, his repertoire even includes a beer flavoured with rose petals. He says he wants to create beers which are new and exciting when compared with the humdrum output of the large Italian breweries.

At Le Baladin brewery, in an area famed for its Barolo wines, brewer Teo Musso produces 'his raptures' using wine and whisky yeasts. His Xyauyu is oxidised for a year to produce a raucous symphony of sherry flavours. He learned to brew in Belgium, and had a spell at the Chimay and Achouffe breweries, and today he makes his own interpretations of some classic beers.

Such is the creativity of Italy's new wave of brewers that it's not uncommon to find brewers from the United Kingdom and United States visiting to find out how to use chestnuts in beer making.

In France many brewers are using their skills to produce beers to reinforce regional and cultural characteristics. While breweries are found all across the country, the two best-known brewing areas are around Strasbourg and Lille in Flanders. The Strasbourg brewers tend to make good, honest interpretations of Germanic lagers. However, the beers of Lille are often wilder, with many brewers specialising in *bieres de garde*. A

▶ **Birrificio Italiano brewer Agostino Arioli turned a passionate hobby for home brewing into an inspirational business.** (Tim Hampson)

▲ **Le Baladin brewery founder Teo Musso harmonises art, science and theatre to produce his "raptures".** (Tim Hampson)

strong pale ale, these beers were traditionally brewed in the winter and spring to avoid the difficulties of fermenting during warm summer days. They're often sold in bottles sealed with a cork.

However, a third region is now honing its own beer identity. Drawing on their Gallic and Celtic heritage, many Bretons are brewing beer as a way of sustaining their identity. Today more than 25 breweries in the region are creating more than 80 artisanal beers. One feature of these Breton beers is the

▼ **Music played through headphones to the fermenting beer at La Baladin is said to influence the character of each brew.**

(Tim Hampson)

diversity of ingredients – from elderberries and honey to herbs, spices and seaweed – that are used to add complexity and depth. A French beer revolution is under way.

The Netherlands might be overshadowed by the neighbouring beer giants of Germany and Belgium, but there's much more to it than the global brewing titan Heineken. The country has a growing number of craft brewers. Producers such as Snab are introducing drinkers to a range of beer styles other than Pilsner, including an American-style pale ale and a *bock*, a style which even has its own annual festival in Amsterdam. The city has two breweries, Brouwerij't IJ and de Prael, producing local brews. IJs has to be the most atmospheric as it's housed within a former bath house next to an old windmill, where drinkers sit on communal wooden benches to enjoy its organic beers. All of its beers are unfiltered, unpasteurised and top-fermented.

In recent years many home brewers in Denmark, Norway, Sweden and Finland have also decided to take the plunge and turn a hobby into a business. Copenhagen, Denmark's capital, has in particular become something of a beer mecca. The city is also home to Carlsberg, one of the world's biggest brewers. The company's contribution to brewing cannot be underestimated, as its legendary brewer J.C. Jacobsen bought back to Denmark a sample of the yeast with which lager was fermented. In the 1840s he made many trips to Germany to learn about cold, bottom-fermenting yeast. He believed that cleaner tasting and clear lager would be more popular in Denmark than the dark ales traditionally produced. When in Munich in 1845 he visited Gabriel Sedlmayr's Spaten brewery, and managed to get a living sample of the yeast. He succeeded in keeping the yeast fresh on his journey back home by placing it in a tin in his hatbox. At every stop on the 600-mile journey home he would find water to cool his precious sample. Then in 1883, as the art and craft of brewing was augmented by science, the legendary brewery scientist Emil Hansen managed to isolate a single-cell pure culture of the yeast.

Finland is home to *sahti*, one of the oldest beer styles in the world. Normally brewed with rye (though sometimes oats are added), the thick beer is filtered through a bed of juniper branches, which imparts sharp, tart, piny and resinous flavours. Some adore the complexity of these ancient beers, others are left confused and bewildered by them. As a beer style *sahti* precedes Europe's industrial revolution and was probably first made by rural workers in medieval times. Traditionally it was made at the start of the summer, as juniper trees came to life again after the long winter.

Conventionally *sahti* is mashed in an old, wooden trough, known as a *kurna*, containing a bed of juniper twigs that acts as a filter and is said to contain many enigmatic wild yeasts, which add to the primitive complexity of the final beer, or more accurately ale (the beer is unhopped). The juniper twigs also act as a preservative and add resin flavours to the final brew.

America's craft beer revolution

The seeds of America's craft beer revolution were sown when a naval technician working on a nuclear submarine somewhere in Scotland developed a taste for British beer, and President Jimmy Carter changed an American law and allowed people to legally brew at home.

On his return to his native California, naval technician Jack McAuliffe studied to be an engineer and taught himself to brew at home. Then in 1976 he decided his hobby should become a business and opened the New Albion Brewery in Sonoma, using his engineering skills to lash together equipment from a former dairy and a soft drinks factory to brew beer.

Today such an event might well go unnoticed, since there are now more than 2,000 craft brewers in the US and thousands more people brewing at home. But New Albion's significance was that it was the first new brewery in California since Prohibition was introduced in 1920.

It's impossible to talk about the development of America's craft brewing revolution without mentioning Prohibition, which ran from 1920–33 and cast a long, dark shadow across the country's brewing industry. When the United States enacted Prohibition the making of beer and wine at home was declared illegal. However, when the legislation was repealed 14 years later a clerical error saw two important words – 'and beer' – left out of the statute which made winemaking legal, and home

▼ **Prohibition, introduced in 1920, put an end to America's then-thriving brewing scene.** (Getty Images)

▲ **Prohibition was a time of much trouble and strife – armed men guard a hidden brewery.** (Getty Images)

brewers had to wait until the Presidency of Jimmy Carter for the legislation to be repealed in 1978.

When Prohibition ended in America in 1933 there were more than 700 breweries in the US, but by the end of the 1970s this had fallen to just 44 companies, and some predicted that within a few years this number would consolidate down to only five. But the legalisation of home brewing launched a creative revolution and thousands took up the hobby. Current estimates indicate that approximately one million Americans are now making their own beer at home.

The pale ale, stout and porter brewed by McAuliffe caused quite a stir, and even attracted the attention of America's national media, intrigued by someone taking on the might of the likes of Budweiser and Miller, who produced cold, fizzy, light lagers.

Any chronicler of the national American beer scene at this time would have found little difference between most of the beers being produced by the industry giants. Most lacked body, few had any aroma of hops, and most were bland on the palate and were intended to be served so cold that drinkers' taste buds could discern nothing. Such differences as there might have been probably weren't even worth noting.

Of the people who started to brew at home, many were inspired by New Albion's impudence at taking on the might of America's corporate brewers. Other had made the pilgrimage to or read about the Anchor Brewing Company in San Francisco, which was bought in 1965 by Fritz Maytag, heir to a washing machine magnate. Maytag was adamant he was going to retain the beer traditions of his brewery. He would not produce a beer that tasted the same as the others on sale. His Liberty Ale, which is full of fruity and floral flavours and has a crisp, entrancing bitterness on the palate, is still regarded as the benchmark for American pale ales.

Sadly New Albion closed in 1982, but the fruits of McAuliffe's revolution were beginning to ripen. From Alaska to Texas, people began brewing without frontiers. All they knew was that their beer shouldn't taste like one of the big national brands. There followed an unconstrained, joyous time when style books were put to one side and boundaries were pushed aside. America was inventing a new world order of beer. The new beers were darker, bitterer and hoppier. Some were inspired by styles from overseas, others were limited only by their brewer's imagination. These beer pioneers brewed with passion and vision, and while drawing on the traditions of the Old World and European traditions they developed a distinct American character of local beers.

The number of craft brewers has risen from eight in 1980 and 537 in 1994 to over 1,600 in 2010, and now stands at more than 2,000, so that most Americans now live within ten miles of a brewery. And many of these craft brewers began their journey by brewing at home.

Brewer Sam Caligone, founder of the Dogfish Head Brewery in Milton, Delaware, started with simple equipment but it helped him develop his ideas for 'off-centered ales for off-centered people'. His beers use unusual ingredients or extreme amounts of traditional ingredients. Muscat grapes, saffron and chicory have all found their way into his kettles. Other brewers, like Garrett Oliver of the Brooklyn Brewery, embarked on missions of their own to show that beer was the perfect partner to good food, and that it was time for wine to leave the stage.

Jim Koch, founder and chairman of the Boston Beer Company, began production of his beers in his kitchen in 1984. Now his company produces two million US barrels of Samuel Adams beers a year. He says: 'One of the best parts about being a brewer at Samuel Adams is that we can truly do anything we can imagine. We're constantly challenged to try new things. A new idea can spring from a recent trip, to a new flavour combination we tried, to a desire to reinterpret a classic style. There's always more to experiment.'

Budweiser might still call itself the 'King of Beers', but many now say the king is dead – long live the craft beer revolution, and that's McAuliffe's legacy.

▲ **Goose Island started life in a Chicago brewpub in 1995 as part of a movement to elevate beer to new heights. It is now owned by AB-InBev.** (AB-InBev)

▼ **The Dogfish Head Brewery started as a simple operation, but is now one of the US's most sophisticated.** (Getty Images)

Beer in Asia and Australasia

John Shore probably thought something along the lines of, 'God it's hot – it's nearly 34°C!' But at least it wasn't as hot or as humid as July, when the temperature could top 40°C. It was October 1793, and Shore was sitting in his new office in Calcutta, where he had just been appointed Governor-General of British India. He was the monarch's representative in the sub-continent.

Regarded by many as a timid man, as he mopped his sweating brow he perhaps pondered how to deal with the many corrupt tax officials who were in his employ. We don't know if he drank beer when he went home to the company of his Indian wife, but if he did the chances are it would have been a pale golden colour.

Even if Shore didn't drink beer, his civil servants certainly did. It's likely that beers brewed in England were sent in casks to India and put into bottles from the first decade of the 18th century, for the civil servants to slake their thirsts. The pale beers of Shore's era could have come from the Hodgson Brewery in London or equally from many others, including the

Bass and Allsop breweries in Burton upon Trent. However, the troops of the East India Company's forces, and the British Indian Army which succeeded it, had other tastes. They preferred the darker porter style, beer historian Martyn Cornell tells me, and they continued to drink it right to the end of the 19th century.

British involvement in India has generated many stories about the origins of a beer known as India Pale Ale, most of which were created during the 20th century, and most of which are nonsense. The stories go that IPAs were stronger, more heavily hopped and only available from the UK. Not so. And that after a ship was wrecked off the coast of Scotland,

◀ **Young hop plants on a plantation at Hops Products Australia – Bushy Park, Tasmania.** (Getty Images)

the people who salvaged its cargo of beer casks got their first taste of this beer style, not previously sold on these islands. There is no evidence for this.

In reality pale ales weren't created for the Indian market. Provided that the malt was of a suitable quality and colour, brewers had actually been brewing pales ales in England since the 17th century, if not before. Also there is no evidence that beers for export were stronger than those drunk in England. Beers of an alcoholic strength of around 6.5% ABV were commonplace, as were heavily hopped beers – though it does seem that at some time during the 19th century brewers exporting beer to a warm climate were advised to add in more hops.

The truth is probably far more prosaic, as pales ales for drinking in India were sold openly in England in 1822, and it seems people really got a taste for IPA after the railways arrived in Burton in 1841 and the bitter beers, which became known as IPAs, were able to be easily transported around the UK.

The story of beer throughout Asia is really the story of European colonisation. While the dominant ingredient used for making alcoholic drinks in the region was rice, with many countries in the region making a variation of sake or Chinese rice wine, wherever the British, Germans and Dutch went, so their beer and breweries followed.

The best-known Australian beer brand in the UK is Foster's lager. Yet it's a beer largely unknown in its home country, with a mere 1% of the Australian beer market. Most Australians prefer to drink the sweet-tasting Victoria Bitter (VB). However, across both Australia and New Zealand there has been a massive growth in the number of microbreweries being set up, contributing to a vibrant beer scene down under. One of the best-known of this new wave is Little Creatures, in Fremantle, Western Australia. Founded in 2000, the company produces US-style hoppy pale ales. Yeast is added to every bottle of its pale ale, letting it ferment right up to the point of drinking.

In China, the Tsingtao Brewery was founded by British and German settlers in 1903. The German soldiers and sailors in Qingdao in particular liked its beers. Today, as befits the country with the largest population, China has the biggest brewing industry, dominated by a small number of massive companies. The country's biggest brand is the locally owned Snow, followed by Tsingtao. However, the world giants of brewing AB-InBev, Heineken and SABMiller all have large stakes in the country.

In Japan, like much of the region, Pilsner-style lager beers dominate the market. However, a change in brewing laws in the 1990s made it easier for small breweries to be established. Inspired by the growing craft brewing movement in the US, a new generation of microbrewers started producing beers in an array of styles, both classic and original. One of the most distinctive is Hakusekikam, which was founded in 1997. Its

▲ **One of Asia's best-known breweries was founded by British and German settlers.** (Getty Images)

brewmaster Satoshi Niwa uses wild airborne yeast to make tart-flavoured ales. The beers are then fermented for a long period, and some are barrel-aged to produce some distinctive beers.

The region might be dominated by multinational companies, but creative brewing isn't dead, and from small towns in Japan to brewpubs in Beijing, Hanoi and Shanghai there are a growing number of small brewers using locally grown ingredients to create inspired brews.

▼ **Giant copper wort kettle at Sapporo Brewery's Beer Museum, Hokkaido, Japan.** (Getty Images)

Beer around the world

Beer is the world's most popular alcoholic drink. It has probably been drunk on every continent in the world, and with today's technology it can be brewed anywhere too. For beer is a product rooted in the soil – be it a beer from a big brewer or a micro, it's made from natural ingredients that have been grown by a farmer. In most cases, but not all, on planet Earth… for beer is also the first alcoholic drink for which one of its ingredients has been grown in space. In 2008, after a five-month mission during which barley was grown for the first time in a Russian laboratory on board the International Space Station, the crop was used by Sapporo Breweries to create 100 litres of Space Barley. The Japanese brewer says that one day it hopes beer will really go extra-terrestrial and become available for astronauts to enjoy in space.

According to the research company Canadean's *Global Beer Trends* report, world beer consumption will soon top two billion hectolitres. Although beer consumption has been affected by economic crises, at a global level growth is still relatively robust, with the market researchers predicting an average growth rate of 2.8%. Two billion hectolitres sounds a lot, but it only requires each of us to drink 30 litres of beer a year.

However, this global headline figure hides differences at a regional level. In Asia, Africa and South America beer consumption is predicted to grow significantly, by more than

5%. Eastern Europe will see an increase of 0.5% while North America will see an increase of just 1.5%. In Western Europe the beer market is expected to marginally decline. By 2015 it's expected that the Chinese will drink one in four of all the beers brewed on the planet.

Nearly half the beers most people drink are brewed by just four massive companies – AB-InBev, SABMiller, Heineken and Carlsberg now account for a combined share of 42% of all beer drunk. And there's another handful of supra-regional companies also competing for people to drink their beers.

But the baldness of the figures hides the fact that a worldwide revolution is going on. There have probably never been more brewers on the planet. From Alaska to the southern tip of South America, from the rolling plains of Hungary to the steppes of Russia, across Asia and Western Europe and all the way to Australia and New Zealand, more and more people are brewing beer and more people are doing it at home, revelling in the enjoyment of creating their own brews.

◀ **Craft beers are now found worldwide – the Szot brewery is located in Santiago, Chile.**
(Getty Images)

The story of the hop

We don't know the name of the brewer who first added hops to beer. But Sharp's head brewer Stuart Howe adds them by the handful to his beer. Lots of them. 'We use them for aroma and to provide bitterness,' he says. 'They also have a preservative quality which stops beer going off.'

There are records of hops being grown in monastic gardens in France and Germany from the 7th century. The plant was valued for its medicinal qualities, and like many plants and spices was added to beer to provide flavour and mask the taste. Any number of herbs and spices could go into the beer in a cocktail of flavours known as 'gruit', which could include henbane, wild rosemary, heather, ginger, spruce, juniper and bog myrtle. Indeed, it's pretty safe to assume that if it grows, a brewer somewhere has probably added it to beer.

However, over time the useful preservative quality of hops became widely recognised, and by the 12th century they were being used by many brewers in what is now Germany and the Czech Republic. By the 14th century commercial cultivation had spread to Flanders.

Trade between England and the Netherlands was brisk, and it's thought that the many Dutch merchants and weavers working in England yearned for the taste of hop-flavoured beer in preference to the probably thicker and sweeter English ale. Up until then 'ale' was a term used to describe a drink made without hops. Then, one day in 1400 on a high tide, a consignment of hopped beer arrived on a cargo boat in Winchelsea harbour in East Sussex.

It's possible that hops may have been used in England earlier. Greenwich Maritime museum houses the remains of an Anglo-Saxon boat which had foundered off Faversham around AD 940. Known as the Graveney long boat, it contains hop residues, suggesting it had carried a cargo across the Channel, though how the hops were intended to be used we do not know.

However, the arrival of the liquid cargo in Winchelsea in 1400 caused quite a stir. The story has it that an angry wrangle broke out over the qualities of unhopped English ale and hopped beer. It was a loud and noisy row which went on for generations. Jingoistic English ale drinkers despised the hoppy beers and railed against the influence of foreigners.

▶ **Once, workers on tall stilts had to string high wires on which hops would grow.** (Beer Genie)

▲ **Hop bines are giant growing plants, but it is only the thumbnail-sized cones which the brewer wants.** (Beer Genie)

Eventually, in 1484, the Brewers' Company – an alliance of ale brewers formed in 1437 – worried about the increasing popularity of beer made with hops, petitioned the Lord Mayor of London that 'no hops, herbs, or other like thing be put into any ale or liquore wherof ale shall be made – but only liquor, malt, and yeast.'

▼ **Many brewers still use dried whole hops in their beers.**
(Cath Harries)

In Norwich, a city where many Flemish weavers had settled, partisan politicians banned the use of hops in 1471. The town of Shrewsbury did likewise in the same year. In 1530 even Henry VIII joined in the row, banning his brewer in Eltham from using hops and brimstone for his ale. Perhaps he was influenced by the makers of gruit, whose trade was being eroded by the use of hops.

Religion too came into the argument, as hops came from the Protestant Low Countries. Consequently ardent Catholics wanted no truck with the hop. The war between ale and beer reached a new low when in 1542 Sussex physician Andrew Boorde wrote that beer was the natural drink of Dutchmen but had recently become much used in England, to the detriment of Englishmen, claiming that it killed those who were troubled with colic. It also 'doth make a man fatte, and doth inflate the belly'. Ale, on the other hand, was the 'natural drynke' of an Englishman.

However, despite the rhetoric people were developing a taste for hoppier and probably lighter beers. Kent's first hop garden was planted by about 1520, and by the middle of the 16th century farmers from the Netherlands were being bought in by the Government to advise English growers on how to cultivate the hop. The tall hop bines grew well and prospered in the fertile soil of Kent. There was also a good supply of wood for the poles up which the hops grew, and to provide the charcoal essential to dry them after harvesting. In fact the growing of hops was so popular, a sure size of the growth of the brewing industry, that legislation was needed to stop farmers giving up their arable fields in favour of hops, which were much more profitable. It was estimated that one acre of hops would make more profit than 50 acres of arable land. In one of the first references to hop growing in England, Thomas Tusser wrote in 1557 that 'hop is worth gold'.

By the end of the 16th century hops had clearly become widely accepted, since in a guide to growing plants and trees published in 1572 Leonard Mascall praises English hops, saying one pound of them will go as far as two pounds of the best hops from beyond the seas.

By 1577 hop growing had reached Herefordshire, where a hopyard was established near Bromyard, near Worcester. After Kent, Herefordshire and Worcestershire were the two great hop growing areas in England. The soil was ideal, and while Kent was close to the large market of London, so Bromyard was close to the expanding city of Birmingham and the brewers of Burton upon Trent.

Despite all of this, for hundreds of years a distinction continued to be made between ale and beer. Even when hops were widely accepted the term ale was used for beers that had a lighter dosage of the green cones, while beers used larger quantities. Often drinkers would mix an ale with a beer, and this practice still persists today – until recently it was very common in London to hear drinkers asking for a light and bitter, meaning a bottle of pale ale mixed with a half pint of draught bitter beer.

The history of malting

All beer is made with a malted grain, usually barley, though any carbohydrate could be used to brew a beer. The role of the malt is to unlock the sweet sugars in the hard grain, which also provides colour and taste to beers. 'Barley is the very heart and soul of beer,' says Warminster Maltings managing director Chris Garret, as he caresses a handful of malted barley before carefully choosing one of the grains and biting into it. 'You can just taste the sweetness and goodness. And it's those sugars the brewer is looking for,' he says. 'Without them we wouldn't have beer.'

▶ **The sweet goodness locked within grain provides beer with its very soul.** (Beer Genie)

Barley has been grown around the town of Warminster in Wiltshire for hundreds of years – the grain thrives on the mixture of clay and silt loams which lie above a layer of chalk – but for centuries many towns and villages in the United Kingdom, especially in England, had their own maltings, very similar in operation though not in scale to Warminster Maltings' traditional floor maltings, which began operation in 1879. Some were small and unprepossessing, others were larger like Warminster, and a few were of considerable size. Indeed, the importance of malting to many communities can still be seen today, as many towns and villages still have dwellings and buildings called the 'malthouse', though the maltster and grain have long since gone.

When the grain arrives at the Warminster maltings it's wetted by Chris and his staff, a process known as steeping. This kick-starts the germination of the grain. To make beer the brewer needs the goodness in the grain – yeast lives on this, and as part of its lifecycle produces alcohol as a by-product.

Once the steeping is completed the grain is laid out on the long floor of the malthouse in a bed 20cm deep. The room soon heats up from the germinating grains, but the maltster doesn't want it too hot, as this will kill the grains; so the maltster controls the temperature by simply opening and closing the windows in the room. Old and former maltings can often be recognised from the outside by their rows of small ventilation windows, with seemingly little space between the different levels. The heat is also dissipated by raking the beds of grain with shovels twice a day. It can be back-breaking work.

When the grains have formed rootlets, the germination has to be stopped. If the growth continues for too long too much of the sugar-sweet goodness that the brewer depends on will be gone. The germinating grain, sometimes known as green malt, is then moved to the floor below, where it's kilned for two days at temperatures in excess of 150°C, and the growing is arrested. The grain is then ready to go to the brewer.

It's unclear when people first started to malt grain. It's likely that our ancestors discovered the benefits of accidental germination, which would have made hard grains edible and pleasant to taste; moreover they could be used in bread and beer making.

In ancient bread- and beer-making the flour of unmalted grain was mixed into a dough, along with sprouted grains, and the mixture would become host to the vital airborne yeast which, when mixed with water, would undergo a natural fermentation, resulting in an intoxicating, nutritious liquid. Archaeologists have found many fragments of pots or jars used for soaking grain.

From this simple technology developed the specialisation of malting, and wooden seeping tanks, floor maltings and

▲ **Beer's journey from the farm to the glass means grain has to be germinated, turned and dried in a maltings.** (Beer Genie)

▼ **During malting, grain needs to be steeped in water to kick-start germination.** (Tim Hampson)

► **Malt can come in many colours and flavours.** (Tim Hampson)

natural draft kilns were commonplace as early as some 1,500 years ago.

By the start of the 19th century there were some very large maltsters in England, mainly in Norfolk and Herefordshire, specialising in producing malt for the growing market for beer in London. The malt was transferred to London either by sea and then up the River Thames to Bear Quay, or along inland waterways such as the River Lee. To achieve economies of scale the bigger brewers established their own maltings. The earlier practice of local communities having their own maltings was probably dealt a mortal blow with the coming of the railway age. The railways opened up the barley fields of the Midlands and East Anglia to the brewing centres of Burton and London.

However, floor maltings weren't that efficient, and by their very nature were dependent on the vagaries of the climate. Barley needs a temperature between 10–16°C to germinate, which makes it hard to do during the hot summer months. Consequently maltsters started to look for new ways to germinate the grain. In the 1870s Galland drum malting – named after its developer, Belgian brewer Nicholas Galland – arrived from the Continent, as did box malting, invented by a Frenchman named Saladin. After steeping the grain was placed in a sealed container through which was passed a constant supply of air at the right temperature and moisture. The grain was turned mechanically or by the passage of air rather than through the sweat and labour of men wielding shovels.

Modern maltings are highly mechanised. They have large fans, computers, furnaces, forced-air and heated kilns. The process has come a long way since the ancient days when people chewed on germinated grains and used the resultant porridge of saliva to create some of the earliest brews.

Visitors to Newton Abbot's oldest company, Tuckers, which began life as a seed merchant in the 1830s before beginning to malt barley in the 1870s, can still see a floor malting in action. This ancient town was a centre for clay mining, and there'd no doubt been many people in the area thirsting for a beer and many brewers keen to secure a supply of quality malt. Consequently Tuckers built its 20m long malthouse here in 1900. Today its malt supplies more than 40 different breweries, including Cornwall's St Austell and the resident Teignworthy Brewery.

A good time to visit is when Tuckers hosts its annual three-day April beer festival. Organised by the area's many small brewers, this features more than 300 different brews, many of which use Tuckers malt. Details are available from Tuckers Maltings, Teign Road, Newton Abbot, Devon TQ12 4AA, or at www.edwintucker.com. Opening hours are normally 10–5 Monday to Saturday, and tour times at the time of writing are 10:45, 12:00, 2:00 and 3:15.

▲ **If malt is made in a traditional maltings, much back-breaking work is often needed.** (Tim Hampson)

▼ **Tuckers, in Newton Abbot, Devon, is a traditional maltings which is open to visitors, and hosts a famed beer festival.** (Tim Hampson)

CHAPTER 2
BEER STYLES

Dancing with the angels

Trying to produce a single list of beer styles upon which everyone can agree is probably as thankless a task as arguing over how many angels can stand on the head of a pin. Many have tried, but no one has succeeded.

History, culture, geography, time and marketing can all influence our perception of a style of a beer. The American Brewers Association (BA) currently lists more than 80 different beer styles, many with extensive sub-divisions. But not one of them is set in stone, and the BA helpfully gives the advice that its list is 'updated yearly with significant changes including editing, deletion and/or addition of beer styles'.

▼ **From bitter to sweet, fruity to malty, the family of beers is an exhilarating exploration of tastes and aromas.**

(John Palmer's Beer Style Spectrum/D. Stickland)

However, we do know that the beer family is large and expanding. The home brewer and beer drinker can choose from an impressive and growing range – ales, lagers, *lambics*, stouts, porters and wheat beers. But it doesn't stop there. Beers made with herbs, spices and fruit can all be found. Some are dark, some are light, some are sweet, some are sour, some are clear, others are cloudy. The extent of the family is limited only by the imagination of the brewers.

However, the family of beer has two broad branches – lager and ale. These two extensive classes are broadly

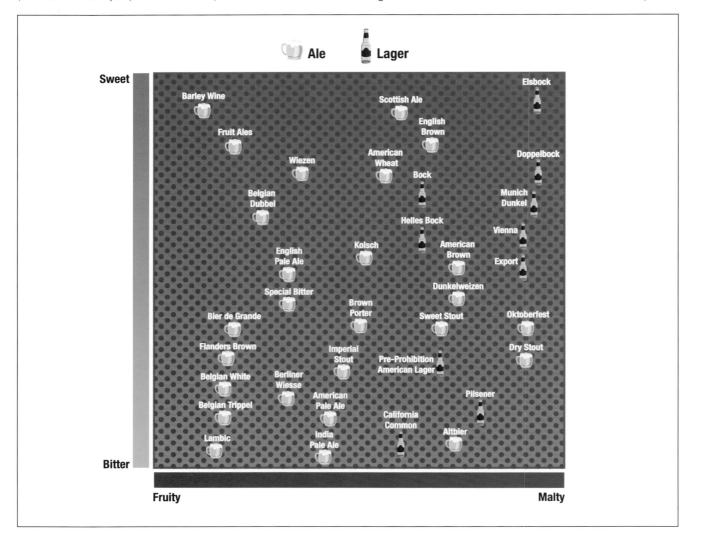

defined by the yeast strain which is likely to have been used during fermentation: *Saccharomyces pastorianus*, which is often called *Saccharomyces carlsbergensis*, is used to make lagers, while *Saccharomyces cerevisiae* is the yeast from which most ales are produced.

Lager is the world's most popular beer style, though it could be argued it's a production process rather than a style. The word 'lager' means to store at a cold temperature, and such beers are traditionally fermented at cooler temperatures than other beers, at between 5–9°C, and then matured or stored at close to freezing, *ie* 0°C – though today some brewers are using warmer fermentation temperatures for their lagers. Lager beers are often described as bottom-fermented, but bottom-cropping would probably be a better description, as during part of its lifecycle the yeast cell feeds off the sugar in the sweet wort, producing ethanol alcohol and carbon dioxide. The yeast ferments at all levels throughout the liquid, but once its work is done it collects at the bottom of the fermenting vessel. Once settled, the brewer can easily drain the beer away, leaving a bed of yeast, and if needed some of this can be 'cropped' for use in the next fermentation.

Ales are traditionally beers that depend on warmer fermentation than lager-style beers, using a yeast that rises to the top of the brewing vessel, where it can be cropped and removed, though eventually it will fall to the bottom. Members of the ale family are typically fermented at 15–25°C.

Top-fermenting (cropping) yeasts are used for brewing ales, porters, stouts, *alts* and *kölschs*, while bottom-fermenting (cropping) yeasts are used for Pilsners, Dortmunders, *märzen* and *bocks*.

Within the family of beers there's also a third broad style – beers which are fermented after exposure to the air, which allows wild yeasts and bacteria to infect them. Some call this natural fermentation, where no selection of yeast has taken place. The resulting flavour is dependent on the actual microorganisms but is normally quite tart and tongue-tingling. The *lambic* beers of Belgium are probably the best-known examples of spontaneous fermentation. Some breweries actually use a commercially available wild yeast, like *Brettanomyces Bruxellensis*, to create more complex beers, often with dry, vinous and some cidery flavours and a tart sourness.

▲ **We encounter many flavours when tasting beers. Start at the centre of the aroma wheel and see if you can work your way out to more detailed descriptions in the outer circle.** (A.Schmelzle)

▼ **There are myriad flavours, aromas and textures in every beer. Try plotting your perceptions on the spikes of the flavour wheel. Place less intense flavours towards the centre.**

(A.Schmelzle/D. Stickland)

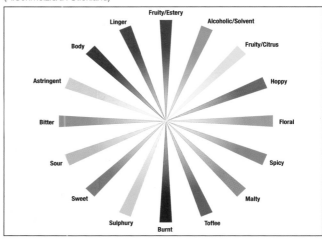

Some members of the beer family

ALES

Alt

Alt is a German word meaning traditional or old. It's a style of beer usually made in Düsseldorf (*alt* beers are often known by the city's name) and a few other cities in northern Germany. It's a dark copper beer, brewed using top-fermentation, which many believe is best drunk in one of Düsseldorf's own brewpubs.

Barley wine

Legend has it that barley wine dates from the 18th and 19th centuries, when England was often at war with France and it was the duty of patriots to drink ale rather than French claret. It's a good story, but… Anyway, barley wines tend to be strong and warming – often between 10% and 12%, though less strong versions are available. Expect boiled sweet and intense dark fruit flavours.

Belgian brown

A traditional beer from the Flanders region of Belgium. This light- to medium-bodied deep copper brown ale typically has a slight to strong lactic sourness and is often known as *Oud Bruin* ('old brown'). *Framboise* variants have raspberries and *kriek* types have cherries added for a second fermentation.

Bitter

Bitter is a blood relative of pale ale and the two descriptions are often used to describe the same beer. Bitter is a child of the industrial revolution in Victorian England. Bitters are generally deep bronze or copper in colour due to the use of slightly darker malts, such as crystal. Part of their commercial appeal was that they could be served quickly on draught, after only a few days of conditioning in the pub.

Bière de garde and saison

Traditional farmhouse beers from the Flanders region of France and Belgium. They can be bottle-conditioned and are often sold in bottles sealed with champagne-style wired corks. The style of beer is characterised by a lightly toasted malt aroma, and some malt sweetness. The hop flavour contribution is likely to be minimal, but not necessarily so. Some sour *Brettanomyces* characteristics can be present. Clove flavours may be detected.

Brown ale

English brown ales are not common in Britain these days, but when found they're likely to be bottled. The colour can range from copper to brown. They have medium body and range from dry to sweet maltiness, with very

little hop flavour or aroma. The roots of this beer could go back to the era before hops were used by English brewers. Brown ales are likely to be darker than a bitter or pale ale, though of course Newcastle Brown Ale is the exception to this rule.

Cask-conditioned ale

Cask-conditioned ales or real ales are unpasteurised living beers, which undergo their secondary fermentation in the container from which the beer is served. A common style in the UK, cask ales are predominantly sold on draught in pubs.

Golden ale

A new style of beer developed in Britain in the 1980s to tempt drinkers away from light-coloured lagers to cask beer. Lighter in colour than a pale ale, lager malts will often be used. Flavoursome hops from America, New Zealand or Australia are often used in abundance. Golden ales are often full of soaring, spicy, citrus flavours. Such beers are frequently served at temperatures lower than 10°C.

Gale ale

Ale flavoured with bog myrtle or sweet gale – which has aromatic leaves – and a host of other herbs was made in Britain until an Act of 1711 brought in a tax on hops and banned any other 'bitter ingredient'.

Green hopped ale

Green hopped ales are hopped with fresh partially dried hops and some undried hops, picked the day the beer is mashed. As the reactive components in the hops haven't been measured in a laboratory the resultant beer is something of a lottery, and achieving a balance with the malt is difficult. Expect fresh flavours.

Imperial stout

A big, bold, giant of a beer, its colour goes from dark copper to black. High in alcohol, it's likely to be rich and malty and can be very sweet. Strong enough to keep for years, the complexity of the beer changes from year to year. Drinking one is never predictable but it is rarely disappointing.

India Pale Ale, US-style

Originally an English pale ale, the style has been reinvigorated and reinvented by the American craft beer movement. American interpretations are often identified by being highly bittered through the massive use of citrus-flavoured hops, which is balanced with rich, juicy malt. Often the signature beer for many brewers, it's now widely brewed by craft brewers worldwide.

Kölsch

Light, almost straw-coloured, this golden ale can officially only be brewed in Cologne in Germany. It's an ale which is served at lager temperatures and is a speciality of many brewpubs in the city. Served fresh, it should be full of light malt and floral fruit flavours; apple or pear characteristic might even be detected.

Mild

Mild was once the most popular style of beer in Britain. It was developed in the 18th and 19th centuries as a less bitter (milder) style of beer than porter and stout, and was the drink of choice for generations of factory and agricultural workers wanting a refreshing drink after a day's work. Often sweet to taste, mild is usually dark brown in colour, due to the use of well-roasted malts or roasted barley, and is lightly hopped.

Milk stout/sweet stout

In the late 19th century a taste arose for sweeter stouts. The perfection around 1907 of stouts made with an addition of

unfermentable lactose sugar, which was originally derived from milk, eventually resulted in one of the most popular British beer styles of the mid-20th century. Now rarely produced, it should have smooth chocolate overtones and be refreshing.

Old ale

Old ale is another style with roots back into beer's distant past. Old ales can mature for months or even years in wooden vessels, where they can pick up some lactic sourness from wild *Brettanomyces* yeasts in the wood. Often known as winter warmers, they can also be matured for long periods in a bottle. They can have flavours of roasted grain, dark soft fruits or even fresh tobacco.

Pale ale

Pale ale was known as 'the beer of the railway age'. Pale ales were developed in Burton upon Trent during the 18th and 19th centuries and were transported round the country first by canal and then by the new railway system. Brewers from London, Liverpool and Manchester built breweries in Burton to make use of the gypsum-rich water to make their own versions of pale ale. One brewer even shipped water to Manchester to brew from. Widely exported, beers sent to India became known as India Pale Ale.

Pale ale, US-style

American pale ales range in colour from deep golden to copper. The style is characterised by floral and citrus American-variety hops like Cascade, though hops from other countries can be used, to produce high hop bitterness, flavour and aroma. American strong pale ales are moderate in their body and maltiness.

Porter and stout

Porter was developed in London and was the first beer to be widely sold commercially, in the early 18th century. As maltsters and brewers grew to understand how to control the roasting of barley to higher temperatures, this brown-coloured beer became darker black and often full of roasted coffee flavours. Lots of hops are usually added for bitterness. The stronger versions of porter were called stout porter, or 'stout' for short.

Rauchbier – smoked beer

A speciality of Bamberg in Germany, the smokiness of these beers derives from the use of malt smoked over beechwood. Alaskan Brewing makes a version with alder-smoked malt. Complex beers, phenolic, banana and cloves flavours are often to the fore. The style pairs well with fatty meats and pickled fish.

Trappist beers

Trappist beers are not a style of beer, though they're all likely to be top-fermenting, bottle-conditioned ales. However, a beer can be described as 'Trappist' if it has been brewed within the walls of a Trappist monastery, either by the monks themselves or under their supervision. Currently, Trappist beers are produced by the abbeys of Chimay, Rochefort, Orval, Westvleteren, Westmalle and Achel in Belgium, Schaapskooi in the Netherlands, and Stift Engelszell in Austria.

Wheat beers, Belgian-style

The Belgian and Dutch versions of wheat beers, which are known as *witte* or *biere blanches*, are usually made with the addition of herbs and spices such as ground coriander seeds and orange curacao or orange peel. The hop presence is normally low, and many believe the roots of the beer go back to medieval times when a herb and spice mixture (gruit) rather than hops was used to flavour beers.

Wheat beers, German-style

Weiss (white) or *weizen* (wheat) beers are made with 40% wheat mixed with barley malt. The style is very common in Germany, especially Bavaria, but it's now a favourite of many home brewers worldwide. Refreshing, crisp and usually turbid, a variation on the ale yeast produces sometimes highly pronounced banana, clove and bubblegum flavours. Unfiltered versions are called *hefeweiss* or *hefeweizen*. Filtered versions are called *kristal*.

Wheat beer variant, Berliner weisse

The lightest of the German wheat beers, *Berliner weisse* is very pale in colour and typically low in alcohol, about 3% ABV. The style was at its most popular in the 19th century, when more than 700 breweries produced it. Today demand has fallen to the extent that it has all but died out in Berlin. Sour to taste, it's often served with flavoured syrups or woodruff.

LAGERS

German-style or Continental Pilsner

The classic German Pilsner is golden or light straw in colour and well hopped. The presence of hop bitterness from the use of noble hops should be medium to high. It is a well-attenuated, medium-light-bodied beer with maltiness present in the aroma and flavour. Some drinkers can often detect sweet corn flavours.

Bohemian or Czech Pilsner

The father of a beer style that's swept the world. The flavour of spicy and herbal hops should sing in harmony with the sweetness of the Moravian Pilsner malt. They can be golden or even pale amber. Some versions of this beer are lagered (*ie* stored) for three months, but many exemplars of the style lager for a much shorter time. The beer should be served with a full, dense, white head.

Helles

A pale lager often brewed around Munich in Germany. Usually light gold in colour, the flavours are far subtler than you'd expect from a Pilsner style.

Dortmunder

Brewed around the German city of Dortmund, this is similar in style to a *helles*. It'll have moderate hop bitterness and not be assertively malty.

Vienna-style lager

Made with a red-coloured Vienna malt, the beer is reddish brown or copper coloured. The malt will dominate the aroma and instil a sweetness into the beer. The hop bitterness will be clean, crisp and relatively low.

Märzen

A seasonal beer from Germany, characterised by a medium body and broad range of colours. Traditionally brewed in March and stored over the summer in ice caves ready for consumption in September.

Bock and its variants

Traditional German *bocks* are strong, malty, medium- to full-bodied, bottom-fermented beers. The complex flavours of malt and fruit usually dominate the taste. *Doppelbocks* are even stronger, and the triple really steps up the excitement. An *eisbock* is one that's made by freezing the beer in a barrel, then taking out the ice to leave a stronger beer. Variants on *bocks* are found throughout the world, particularly in Belgium.

American-style lager

Light in body and very light to straw in colour, American lagers are very clean and crisp and heavily carbonated, and are usually served very cold. The flavour components should be subtle but complex, with no one ingredient dominating. Malt sweetness is light to mild. Corn, rice, or other grain or sugar adjuncts are often used. Hop bitterness, flavour and aroma are negligible to very light.

WILD BREWS

Lambic

Unblended, naturally and spontaneously fermented *lambics* are intensely sour, and sometimes, but not always, acetic. They're very, very dry. *Lambic* is a beer which traditionally is made in Belgium's Senne Valley. Once all beers would have been fermented in this fashion. The beer is traditionally matured in oak barrels to produce its compelling flavours. Old hops are used for preserving the beer, not bittering it. A *lambic* will often pair unbelievably well with food.

Gueuze lambic

Old *lambic* is blended with newly fermenting young *lambic* to create this beer. Light-bodied, milder and sweeter than a single *lambic*, many people find it a more approachable beer. Additional sugar is sometimes added to the beer to help counter the acidity. If brown sugar is added the beer is known as a *faro*.

Fruit lambic

Often soft fruit such as raspberry or cherry will be added to a *gueuze*, but pear and blackcurrant and even banana have also been used to create these beers. Often fermented in a wooden cask, in traditional versions most of the sugars are fermented out and the beer is very dry. Some versions use fruit syrup, which often overpowers the beer's acidity.

Leipzig-Gose

A beer that's traditional to the Leipzig area of Germany. Traditionally they're spontaneously fermented, similar to Belgian-style *lambic* beers. They're drunk young, and drinkers should expect acidic lemon or other citrus-like flavours on the nose and palate. There's normally little evidence of hops or malt character.

SOME OTHER BEERS

Rye beer

Rye beers, known as *roggenbier* in Germany, are brewed with a proportion of rye malt. Usually dark in colour and low in hops, the beers have spicy and fruity flavours. The taste of the rye is often present in the finished beer.

Fruit beer

Fruit beers are any beers that use fruit or fruit extracts in either the mash, boil, primary or secondary fermentation.

Pumpkin beer

Popular with brewers in the US, such beers use pumpkins as an adjunct in either the mash, boil, primary or secondary.

Sake-yeast beer

A beer brewed with sake yeast. The colour will depend upon the malts used. Sake yeast, which can be slow to ferment, often produces strawberry or melon esters. The challenge for the brewer is to find a hop cocktail that can harmonise with the fruitiness.

Wood- and barrel-aged beer

A wood- or barrel-aged beer is one that's been aged for a period of time in a wooden barrel or in contact with wood. This beer is aged with the intention of imparting the particularly unique character of the wood and/or what's previously been in the barrel. New wood is likely to add vanilla flavours. Used sherry, rum and whisky casks and other barrels can be used, contributing to some unique and complex flavours.

A home brewer's journey

It's been quite a journey for Hobsons Brewery. In 20 years a hobby as a homebrewer has been converted into a thriving business, which has gone from strength to strength. Yet, even though the business is a success, its founding principle of being a local brewer, serving its own community, remains untarnished.

When father and son Jim and Nick Davis founded the brewery in 1993, some would have considered them mad. At the time beer consumption and production was falling. However, the pair were convinced there would be a market for locally produced, artisanal beer, and that people would turn away from mass-market lagers and keg beers.

At the time, Jim and Nick were part of a new wave of entrepreneurs setting up their own breweries. Few could have predicted how successful the movement would become, as there are now more than 1,000 in the UK, and the numbers seem to be rising on an almost daily basis.

▼ **Craft brewing is a hands-on process at Hobsons.**
(Hobsons Brewery)

Late in 1992 Jim and Nick started to look for a reasonably priced unit or building to rent, and after months of searching South Shropshire the only suitable site was found to be a former sawmill in Cleobury Mortimer.

The ethos behind the new company was to embrace the provenance of the area to produce wholesome real ale. Shropshire has always been a firmly independent county, which is why it can now support at least 17 microbreweries.

The biggest fillip to the microbrewery sector came from the campaigning work of the craft brewers' trade association SIBA, which persuaded the Government to introduce progressive beer (PBD) duty in 2002. Brewers producing less than 60,000 hectolitres a year now get a favourable tax break on excise duty. Indeed, some regard it as then Chancellor Gordon Brown's best moment, as brewers producing less than 5,000hl of beer became eligible for a flat 50% reduction in beer duty. While a large brewer pays 50p a pint for a 5% ABV beer, a small pub brewery only pays 25p.

The introduction of progressive beer duty meant that many small brewers were able to create a war chest of capital, which they could invest in staff, equipment, marketing and pubs.

In recent years Hobsons has gone from strength to strength, winning multiple awards for its cask ales and green accolades for its sustainable thinking, while continuing to invest in its business. The old second-hand brewing kit has long-since gone. While the overall beer market still continues to fall, production at Hobsons, like many other small brewers, continues to rise.

The Shropshire brewery now offers five cask ales, but the backbone of its product continues to be its original brew, Best Bitter, a hoppy bitter of 3.8% strength. However, its big break came a few years back when its Mild was named as the best beer in Britain by the Campaign for Real Ale. Then on its 20th anniversary the company's original brew, Hobsons Best Bitter, took the title of Champion Bitter in the West Midlands. Nick said: 'This is a very special award for us, not only has our original beer been crowned a Regional Champion, we're also very proud that this is a locally produced pint, with the hops grown in Worcestershire and Herefordshire and the barley harvested within 30 miles of the brewery. All part of our ethos to source locally and set up a network of local growers.'

Hobsons Brewery is at Newhouse Farm, Tenbury Road, Cleobury Mortimer, Shropshire DY14 8RD. Website: www. hobsons-brewery.co.uk.

▲ Former home brewers, and the founders of Hobsons Brewery, Jim and Nick Davis.

(Hobsons Brewery)

▼ The men behind the beer, outside the Kings Arms in Cleobury Mortimer, which received the first delivery of a barrel of Hobsons Best Bitter in 1993. Left Richard Farquharson, barley-grower, of Seisdon, Wolverhampton; middle Rob Higginson, Hobsons' original brewer; and right Geoff Thompson, hop-grower, of Little Lambswick Farm, Lindridge, Tenbury Wells. (Hobsons Brewery)

Thornbridge Brewery support home brewing

Never ordinary, art and science work hand in hand at the Thornbridge Brewery, where some of the UK's most innovative beers are created.

For owner Jim Harrison it was a love of football that provided the inspiration for him to set up a brewery at his home, Thornbridge Hall in Ashford in the Vale, Derbyshire. As an ardent supporter of Sheffield Wednesday his love of real ale took him to the Fat Cat pub, owned by lifelong Sheffield United fan Dave Wickett. He had heard of Dave's reputation for selling and brewing good beer at the Kelham Island Brewery in Sheffield. And it's quite a reputation, as within 15 short years of establishing Kelham Island the former economics lecturer, who died in 2012, had garnered a sack-ful of awards for the quality and innovation of his brews – including the coveted Campaign for Real Ale Champion Beer of Britain Award in 2004 for Pale Rider.

As director of Sheffield Wednesday supporters' club the Owls Trust, Jim Harrison was always looking for ways to raise funds for the club – and he saw the success of Dave Wickett's brewing enterprise and his ability to produce special brews to celebrate events in the city of Sheffield as something of which he could take advantage. Jim wanted his football team to have its own beer, which could be bought by the Wednesday fans, thereby raising money for the club. The beer was brewed for him at the Kelham Island Brewery, but Jim soon realised that he now wanted to brew his own beers in his own brewery.

At the time Jim Harrison and his wife Emma had just bought Thornbridge Hall. 'The next step had to be to serve my own beer in my own bar,' recalls Harrison, 'reviving the tradition once common of country house brewing.' So in 2005 he opened his own brewery located in an old stonemason's and joiner's workshop.

Many of Britain's new wave of craft brewers are content with brewing traditional English bitters, but brewing ordinary beers isn't something that's within the Thornbridge repertoire. The philosophy of the Thornbridge brewers is to brew small batches of original beers using the finest raw materials. Some, like the heavily hopped Jaipur IPA and full-bodied St Petersburg Stout, draw on historical beers; but for others, local plants, fruits and herbs have been used, such as

▼ **Brewing ordinary beers isn't within the repertoire of Thornbridge owner Jim Harrison.** (Tim Hampson)

Within a few short years, Thornbridge has created an astonishing range of interesting beers. (Thornbridge)

elderflower and nettle beers, to add new flavours to beer's chorus of tastes. One beer used an Italian honey, made by bees that had feasted upon chestnut blossom. And the latest Thornbridge creations include beers stored in wooden barrels that have been used to store different whiskies. The brewery's St Peter's Imperial Russian Stout was conditioned in three different whisky barrels from Speyside, Highland and Islay. The results are three beers of marvellous intensity from the whiskies, with the individual characteristics of each whisky giving something to the beers. The Speyside Reserve has a dry, herbal edge, with an astringent finish; the Highland Reserve has a sweeter, grassy palate; and the Islay Reserve has a bold, peaty and marvellously smoky finish.

In 2009 a new 30-barrel, state-of-the-art brewery and bottling line was built at nearby Bakewell to meet growing demand and increase the product range. Harrison says: 'From the beginning at Thornbridge we knew that excellence and quality of process and product would be paramount to our success and delighting drinkers. Our vision was to create products that would make us one of the leading new breweries in the UK. The adoption of the "Innovation, Passion and Knowledge" strapline for the brewery was no hollow promotional stunt but a cultural statement of how, through our many activities, we would go about our day-to-day business.'

Thornbridge now operates from two brewery sites. The original Hall is about experimentation and barrel-aging and creation, including premium bottled products, whereas the contemporary Riverside brewery highlights the company's ability to innovate through technology. 'We enjoy making our beers and have a lot of fun doing so,' says Harrison.

Since 2011 the company's passion for beer and the people who make it has extended to home brewing, following the launch by Thornbridge Brewery together with home-brew supplier BrewUK and pub operator Nicholson's Pubs, of the inaugural Great British Home Brew Challenge. Over 100 entries were submitted, covering a range of beer styles.

The competition proved a great success and a brilliant showcase of the emerging talent in the British home-brewing scene. Paul Carruthers' 'Frank as Apollo', a 4.6% premium bitter, emerged as the winner and was then brewed at Thornbridge and enjoyed across Nicholson's 80 pubs. Thornbridge's head brewer Rob Lovatt said: 'I developed my own passion for making beer through homebrewing in my parents' garage. Hopefully this competition can help to inspire some of the next generation of new and innovative brewers coming through in the UK's expanding craft beer scene.'

Homebrewer Paul Carruthers was blown away by the news that he'd won the award. 'I'm well aware of the high standard of home-brewed beer and so I was completely overwhelmed. To have one of my recipes brewed was an absolute dream come true.'

Paul had only started brewing in 2008. Before that, he says, he only drank premium lager, and thought he'd try and brew some beer like that at home. 'My first kit brew was foul,' he said, 'but gave me the incentive to find out more, so I joined an online forum and discovered "all grain" brewing, which fascinated me. The combination of art and science involved pushes all of my buttons, and when the result is beer, there is no downside.

'It's alchemy! I built a brewery from an old copper water tank that we'd removed from the bathroom. I sawed it in half to make a boiler and mash tun, and I was off. Since then I've had a bash at a lot of beer styles, but there's still an enormous amount left to learn.'

Pilsen Urquell, the town that gave its name to Pilsner

Pilsener, Pilsner or pils are the names often given to the most famous lager style in the world; and the spiritual birthplace of what is claimed to be the world's first bright golden beer is the city of Plzen in Bohemia in the Czech Republic. Pilsner Urquell wasn't the first golden lager, as is often claimed, but it has become the template for a style of beer that's since been brewed worldwide. However, few of the pretenders to the Pilsner crown come close to the complexity of the original Pilsner. A true Pilsner requires maturation time to develop its clean, crisp flavour and assertive hop characteristics, which are a million miles away from the mass-produced pale imitations that dominate the world beer market.

Czech beers were probably cloudy and brown in colour until 1842, when Josef Grolle from Bavaria was contracted by Martin Stelzer, founder of the Burgher's Brewery of Pilsen, to brew a beer which could rival the new style of copper-coloured beers then emerging from Vienna. Until this time beer in the town had probably been brewed using a top-fermenting yeast. However, Grolle – who had a reputation for rudeness – bought a German lager yeast with him, which according to legend was smuggled into the country. With this he created a fresh, clear, golden beer,

▼ **Elegant gates mark the entrance to the magic of Pilsner Urquell brewery.** (Tim Hampson)

topped with a wispy, snow-white head. It was ideal for serving in the newly developed mass-produced clear glassware that was becoming widely used. The crystal clarity of the beer was made possible by advances in malting in which direct heat from hot coals, always difficult to control, was replaced by warm air, making it easier to produce paler shades of malt.

The beer was a sensation. Cold-fermented, it's full of sweet flavours from the Bohemian or Moravian barley and spicy Zatec hops, often known by their German name Saaz. The Saaz hops impart an especially fresh herbal aroma and contribute to a certain and classy finish. A true Pilsner, at 4.4% ABV, has a moderate amount of alcohol, whereas most

beers from Continental Europe typically have an alcoholic strength of 5.0% ABV. The unfermented sugar in the beer contributes to its assertive richness.

The grandiose entrance to the brewery exudes a confident swagger and pride in the work that takes place inside. It's like a two-arched mini-version of the Brandenburg Gate. Architecturally the brewery's buildings – a mixture of old and new, of Gothic, Baroque and modern minimalist – look as if they'd be just as much at home in a Disney theme park. The skyline is dominated by a water tower that looks like it's a minaret from *The Arabian Nights*. At one end there's even an old steam engine and railway lines, which were once used to bring malt into the brewery and take beer to Vienna and even further afield. The brewery's rapid expansion was enabled by developments in refrigeration, which enabled beer to be easily transported far and wide without loss of character.

The brewery takes its low-sulphite, low-carbonate water from its own springs, which through serendipity is ideal for Pilsner production. The brewery was built on the bank of the Radbuza River, directly above a sandstone foundation that was easily carved with tunnels for cold storage, or lagering, of this new style of beer. Once the beer was fermented in open vessels made of Bohemian oak. The brewery had more than 1,000 of them, each capable of holding more than 30hl. The scale of the fermentation vessels was matched by a maze of underground galleries containing more than 3,500 large, pitch-lined oak casks, where slowly, slowly, in the cold, damp conditions, the beers matured from a precocious brew into one with a majestic fullness.

▲ **A bold, confident elegance can be seen all around the brewery's Plzen site in Bohemia.** (Tim Hampson)

Today the wooden vessels have been replaced by the elegance and efficiency of steel, and Pilsner Urquell's master brewer Václav Berkais is convinced that his predecessor Josef Grolle would have also used steel rather than wood had it been available. Large, graceful, copper-coloured vessels dominate the brewing hall, but there have been few

▼ **Pilsner Urquell's brewing hall is a place of remarkable beauty.** (Tim Hampson)

other changes in the production of Pilsner Urquell's beer. It continues to use a triple decoction mash, as it has for over 75 years, portions of which are drawn off at three different times over the course of more than four hours. Each portion, or decoction, is heated, then boiled briefly. The process helps break down the complex carbohydrates in the malt into simpler, fermentable sugars.

The old Pilsner brewhouse is now converted to a visitor centre. Here can be found a replica of a malt store and some used, gleaming coppers, as bright and shiny as the first day they were commissioned. There's also a sensory recreation of the brewing process where visitors can see, touch, smell and taste the ingredients of beer. Tours of the brewery allow visitors to see some of the 10km of labyrinthine underground cellars, where once the beer was lagered (stored) for long periods in wooden barrels lined with pitch. Walking through these dimly lit and ice-cool sandstone cellars, where filtered and non-pasteurised Pilsner Urquell can be sampled, poured straight from the barrel, is the highlight of the tour. Drinking unfiltered Pilsner in its home town, underneath the original brewery, has to be one of the great experiences of any beer traveller. It's just perfection in a glass.

◄ **Drinking unfiltered Pilsner straight from the barrel is the highlight of a brewery tour.** (Tim Hampson)

▽ **The full range of Pilsner Urquell's beers can be found in the brewery's busy tap.** (Tim Hampson)

Brewing a Trappist beer at Orval

In the world of beer there are, indeed, many God-blessed brews, but the best must be those from the Trappist breweries.

Breweries can only use the Trappist appellation if the beers have been brewed within the enclosed community of a monastery and the monks have an element of control over the process. The term Trappist is a designation of origin rather than a style, though there are some shared characteristics between all the monastic brews. The magnificent abbeys where monastic brewing takes place are Achel, Chimay, Orval, Rochefort, Westmalle and Westvleteren in Belgium, Koningshoeven in the Netherlands, and Stift Engelszell in Austria. All the brewing abbeys share a common commitment to quality. The monastic communities pride themselves on using the very best ingredients and the highest-quality brewing equipment.

Between them, the monks and their secular workers produce more than 20 beers. All are top-fermenting, likely to be strong and bottle-conditioned, and full of yeast, with fruity and aromatic flavours. However, the beers from Orval, which is owned and run by Cistercian monks, are light and dry. They're made with three Belgian malts and white candy sugar, and have a distinctive pale orange hue. Sacks of dry hops – Styrian Goldings – are added to the beer while it completes its secondary fermentation. These add balance to the brew and give the beer a rich, round, earthy, sweet aroma.

According to legend the monastery was established when Countess Mathilda of Tuscany lost a golden ring in a lake in

▲ **The Orval Abbey is home to one of the world's greatest breweries.** (Tim Hampson)

◣ **A redundant, but still shining brewery copper marks the entrance to the town of Chimay.** (Tim Hampson)

◢ **A monk oversees bottling at Rochefort.**
(Tim Hampson)

◀ **Bags of hops wait to be used at the Orval brewery.** (Tim Hampson)

1070. She promised that if it were found she would thank God by building an abbey. The ring was brought to the surface by a trout and Mathilda said, 'Truly this place is a *val d'or*', or golden valley. A ring and trout are shown on the Orval label and on many images in the brewery.

Brewing myth will have you believe that monks have been brewing beers continuously from medieval times. It's a good story, which omits the Reformation and the fact that many monasteries were abandoned and used as a source for building stone by local people for centuries.

It was actually in 1926 that the de Harenne family, who had acquired the Orval ruins and surrounding lands in 1887, donated them to the Cistercian order so that monastic life could be re-established there. Then in 1931 the monks took the decision to begin brewing again as a way of raising money for the order and its charitable activities. The brewery's search is not for profit but a *redevance* – that is, enough funds left over from commercial activity so that money can be spent on the upkeep of the abbey, the local community and overseas projects. Each Trappist brewery, whatever its capacity might be, only produces enough beer to meet its financial needs.

Orval director Francois de Harenne says: 'The monks take a view of the long-term and want the very best equipment. The tradition of Trappist breweries is for the equipment to be sophisticated. We have a high level of quality and we must keep it. We're not free to sell a second grade, inferior product.'

The Orval brewery is unique in using *Brettanomyce* yeast. Unlike many wild yeast brewers who use spontaneous fermentation to get the 'Brett' soured characteristic, the Orval brewers inoculate their beer with 'Brett' at bottling. Essentially this means that Orval goes through a small additional fermentation in the bottle with wild yeast.

◀ ◀ **The beer is indeed Godly blessed at Orval.** (Tim Hampson)

◀ **Legend has it that the Orval abbey was founded after a trout found the lost wedding ring of the Countess Matilda of Tuscany.** (Tim Hampson)

The origins of this very distinctive beer can probably be attributed jointly to German brewer Martin Pappenheimer and Belgians Honoré Van Zande and John Vanhuele, who were employed at the brewery. Together they produced a beer that's influenced by both German and British brewing techniques.

Many beers change with age, but none change quite like Orval. Young Orvals are characterised by a fresh hop bouquet, fruity esters and a pronounced bitterness. But after nine months Orval undergoes a complete change. The once fresh hop bouquet turns into an old-fashioned hop aroma and the pronounced bitterness fades as caramel malt flavours become more prominent. Although 'Brett' may start to show before the beer is nine months old, it really starts to shine after this time. Served without sediment, a beer of six months or more has a particularly bright appearance.

The grounds of Orval Abbey are open to the public, but sadly the brewery isn't. However, its beers, including the Petit Orval, which is the beer the monks can drink, can be bought from the adjacent Ange Gardien pub.

▲ **Trappist breweries insist on using the very best equipment and ingredients.** (Tim Hampson)

▼ **A traditional bar close to Orval is a perfect place to relax and try the beers.** (Tim Hampson)

CHAPTER 3
BEER APPRECIATION

The best way to enjoy a beer is to be in good company. The joyful sipping of a brilliant brew has fuelled many a good conversation. Beer indeed is a social lubricant. It's much more than an alcoholic liquid in a glass, and is one that with a little more knowledge can be enjoyed even more.

TASTING

Take your time, but don't wait too long or the beer could become flat and lose its aroma. All the senses should be involved when you're enjoying a beer:

Sight

We drink with our eyes – our visual sense whets the appetite and sets the taste buds anticipating. What's the colour of the beer – light, dark, cloudy or crystal clear? Is it golden or black? Does the beer have a head and what does it look like? Does the beer have a big collar of foam on top or is it tight, discrete and somewhat more restrained? And are there bubbles of carbon dioxide rising up the beer? The answers to these lip-smacking questions are an indicator to the style of the beer and can be an indicator of its condition. Great beers always look good in the glass. And great beers served well will usually leave a trace of foam or lacing on the inside of the glass as you drink.

Touch

What temperature is the glass? Each beer has an optimal serving temperature, which is probably somewhere between 4–11°C. But stronger ales can be warmer: the higher temperature releases soaring fruity aromas and esters enhancing the beer flavour. But a cool crisp Pilsner needs to be served cooler or the taste will be killed and its piquant delicacy muted. The glass temperature is important. Too warm, straight out of a dishwasher for instance, will result in a disappointing experience.

Smell

Given how sensitive our noses are, we really don't look after them. They can detect and discriminate between a myriad of aromas – there are more than 1,000 – and pick up so many tastes that our tongue can't detect. If the beer is a Pilsner can you detect some flowery notes? If it's a rich, dark stout is there a hint of coffee? On a barley wine you might detect some swirling winey, almost sherry-like aromas. A cloudy, yellow German wheat beer should release a flourish of bubblegum flavours. Are there whirls of citrus flavours from the hops used? For just a moment resist taking a sip and let the aromas swirl and your nose do its work.

Taste

Take a sip and let it work its way around your mouth and then swallow. Spread around our mouths are an array of sensitive taste buds. They can detect salt, sweet, bitter, sour and umami. A common misconception is that certain parts of the tongue can only detect certain tastes. Not so, though certain areas may be more susceptible to certain sensations than others. Some beer can play tricks – a hoppy aroma may not always follow through in the taste. But is the beer fruity – can you detect dark fruit flavours or even a hint of malted biscuits? The feel of the beer in your mouth is also important. Does it feel good on your tongue? Is there a satisfying level of bitterness? And don't forget to swallow. Ideally there should be a slow warming feeling as the beer is swallowed, which should linger, but not for too long, at the back of the throat.

Sound

The clink of glasses with fellow drinkers is a way of bringing sound, our last sense, into beer appreciation. Just as good are a few words of heartfelt appreciation. Let your feelings unfurl from deep within your soul: 'That was good! I think I'll have another.'

Beer Genie

Beer Genie

Beer and food matching

Beer is a wonderful companion to food, and like wine the attributes of a beer can be used to complement or contrast with the tempos and textures of food.

Yet there's a long-held expectation that only wine can partner the finest food. But try to find a wine to partner the stringency of a blue cheese, or the fragrant citrus favours of goat's cheese. And is there a wine that will work with a spicy curry, or even pickle? So, there are in fact many occasions when only beer is best. Anyone who's ever tasted the contrasting combination of fresh oysters and stout knows that a sparkling wine is a mere affectation.

The Belgians have for many years held beer and food pairing in high esteem indeed, and the gastronomic repertoire of Belgian cooking dates back to medieval times. With so many different styles of Belgian beer there's tremendous scope to fully exploit their flavour through eating and drinking. We wrongly say that Belgium is boring. It's actually a land of many beers, and chefs wanting to pair them with regional delicacies.

Kwinten De Paepe is head chef at the Trente restaurant in Leuven. Beer is always within his reach in his restaurant – not for drinking himself, but to use in his award-winning dishes or

Beautiful Beer

◀ **Fruity beers pair beautifully with desserts.** (Beer Genie)

as an accompaniment to his fine menu. 'Don't underestimate the culinary power of beer,' he says. He is adamant that 'a well-chosen beer gives a classic dish a completely different dimension. It gives taste, aroma and personality to a dish.'

His favourite beer to work with is *gueuze*. He says the complex, mildly acidic taste to old *gueuze* is a gift to any chef. 'It's delicious with pork if you use it with mustard. White beer gives starters a fresh acidic accent. Brown beers in turn give desserts a sweet, slightly bitter and caramelised taste. Beer is so versatile,' he says.

In England the British Guild of Beer Writers has been pairing beer and food for 25 years at its sumptuous annual dinners. At the most recent, award-winning chef Simon Young partnered baked black cod in miso and mirin with Windsor and Eton's sparkling Pilsner-style beer Republika. The main course of roast Norfolk partridge, hotpot of braised leg, sweet and sour braised red cabbage and blackberry Mauldons porter game jus was paired with Hall & Woodhouse's Champagne Woodwose. The bottle-conditioned beer, served from a champagne-style bottle, was stored upright for 72 hours to ensure the sediment settled to the bottom before being served at room temperature in a champagne glass. For the dessert course, chilled vahlrona chocolate fondant, banana yogurt ice cream and fresh honeycomb was paired with Hook Norton's Double Stout, and finally Innis and Gunn's Raspberry beer was partnered with some petit fours.

Sriram Aylur, head chef at the Michelin-starred Aylur of Quilon in London, has introduced the UK's first Vintage Beer List, taking the concept of beer and haute cuisine to a new level. Based in London's Victoria, around the corner from Buckingham Palace, Quilon is already acclaimed internationally for its five- and eight-course beer menus paired with its south-west coast Indian dishes, and for its international beer list. The new Vintage Beer List offers eight different vintages of Fuller's Vintage Ale.

Sriram is passionate about matching beer to food. He believes that in the UK too much attention has been given to wine by the media, when beer is our national drink. He says: 'We need to bring beer back to the front, simply because there are so many beautiful beers produced. Typically, I've seen people go into a pub and say "give me a lager", which means nothing. That's not something you do with wine, or even tea. You don't just say "give me a tea" – you ask for an Earl Grey, or a green tea, or something else. So I think beers need to be respected the same way, if not better, because they're very varied in taste, experience, feel and flavour.' Sriram is no stranger to preparing food for big events, as once a year he prepares a beer banquet for heads of state at the G7 talks in Davos, Switzerland.

The chic Cinnamon Club in London offer a 'Beer &

▶ **A well-chosen beer takes fish-and-chips to new heights.**
(Beer Genie)

Spice' menu that pairs no less than six modern Indian dishes with six thirst-quenching beers. Highlights include tandoori paneer tikka with red onion and pepper paired with Californian Sierra Nevada Pale Ale; lamb seekh kebab with mint and yoghurt paired with Belgian brew Maredsous Brune; and stir-fry of shrimps with chilli and apricot paired with Daylight, a cocktail of tequila and Chambord topped with the Spanish beer Moritz.

The internationally known London restaurant Galvin at Windows recently tried out a beer menu. The Michelin-starred restaurant, on the 28th floor of the London Hilton, Park Lane, combined its award-winning cuisine with a selection of beers from Camden, Timothy Taylor, Kernel, Fuller's, Jennings and Samuel Smith breweries. Pairings included slow-cooked pork belly with Kernel India Pale Ale or Fuller's Vintage Ale 2004. A Camden Hells lager was served with a dish of mussels and smoked haddock. Head chef André Garrett said: 'Britain is renowned worldwide for the quality of its beer, so what better way to experience its diversity and style than alongside the quality of our Michelin-starred dishes?'

Also in Britain, top Michelin-starred restaurants such as Le Gavroche, Le Manoir aux Quat'Saisons and Aubergine have inspirational beer lists. At Le Gavroche in London chef Michel Roux Jr serves Liefmans Kriek cherry beer with his spicy seared tuna dish. The list includes Kasteel Cru, a champagne yeast-fermented aperitif from Flanders, Rochefort 8, a strong pudding-friendly Trappist beer from Belgium, and the refreshing Kronenbourg 1664.

In America many chefs both cook with beer and match it to foods. The Higgins restaurant in Portland, Oregon, carries a beer list that would be the envy of many a Belgian bar. Higgins' cooking focuses on Pacific Northwest ingredients and traditional French techniques, incorporating an eclectic range of influences from around the world. Presentations, textures and flavours are intense and sophisticated, yet uncontrived. The meat, smoked seafood and cheese platters are paired with Belgian and German beers or something from local craft brewers.

Brooklyn Brewery's brewmaster Garret Oliver says that beer can be paired with all kinds of food. He thinks every upmarket restaurant should carry a beer list as well as one for wine, so that people can discover for themselves that beer is an admirable, deserving companion to the finest food.

At the upmarket, upscale Gramercy Tavern in New York diners can pair a scallops, mussels and clams dish with a sour Jolly Pumpkin wheat beer or a heart steak with Stone's Sublimely Self Righteous Black IPA.

▶ **Beers can be paired with all kinds of foods – and occasions.**
(Beer Genie)

Beer as an ingredient in cooking

Beer has a long and celebrated culinary history. Exalted dishes like Welsh rarebit, carbonnades and fondues all owe their character to various types of beer. In Britain both the Georgians and the Victorians widely used beer as an ingredient.

Modern thinking chefs understand that beer has certain characteristics that excite their culinary taste buds. It adds a marvellous lightness to batters, its natural carbonation produces bubbles that can dance vivaciously across the tongue, which can raise even the most stolid of accompaniments. This is why beer can be used in recipes for Christmas and winter puddings, and many batters, breads and cakes. Even ice creams and sorbets will benefit from its sparkling presence. If it's used as a marinade it's less overwhelming than a robust red wine, which can dominate a boeuf bourguignon.

Once the alcohol in beer has been evaporated during cooking it leaves behind a subtle hint of barley and hops that helps bring out the simple, natural flavours that so many modern chefs are seeking.

As an ingredient in the kitchen the importance of beer is its versatility and range of tastes, aromas, colours and textures. From the lightness of a good Pilsner and the hearty joy of an English IPA, through to the more robust Belgian ales and the profound joyous boisterousness of a stout, beer lends itself well to almost any recipe. It can be used as a marinade and will tenderise raw fish or braised meat. Bolder beers can add colour to a sauce or intensity to a soup. Beer is more than a substitute for wine. In a dressing it can be poured over fruit, or added to the cooking water when boiling a ham.

Beer and... chocolate?

Chocolate is often described as the food of the gods. If that is so then its pairing with beer must take it to an even more sublime level. If heaven has a glass ceiling then beer and chocolate must smash through it.

Perhaps their tongue-tingling affinity comes from the fact that they share a basic taste – bitterness – which comes from the hops in beer and the cocoa beans in chocolate. And then there's a shared sweetness from chocolate's sugar and the malted barley used to make beer.

A dark Belgian chocolate works wonderfully with Brooklyn Brewery's Imperial Stout or a tart *gueuze*. A chilli truffle pairs deliciously with an exquisite Sierra Nevada IPA, and organic dark chocolate is a perfect partner to Hook Norton's Double Stout.

Sometimes it's the simplest artisanal combinations that allow great beers to shine. The Czechs love smoked pork and hams. Basted with glasses of dark lager, the beer adds a glorious sweetness to the meat. And in Britain what could be better than the joyous harmony of a glass of English ale and the simplicity of good bread and a strong unpasteurised Cheddar cheese? Beer and food are a passionate combination.

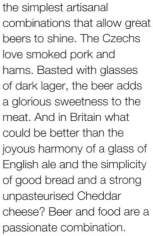

◀ In Bamberg, Germany, try pairing hearty meat dishes with locally brewed smoked beers. It's heaven!

(Tim Hampson)

Beer Genie

A guide to matching beer and food

There are no strict rules about beer and food matching. It's entirely down to what you like and enjoy. However, there are a few basic principles that need to be kept in mind.

Firstly, complement or contrast. Usually one looks to partner a beer with a food that has a complementary taste – big, bold IPAs go well with robust stews, for instance – but contrasts work too; a stout is a sublime partner to an oyster. A crisp but not too sweet lager goes well with creamy dishes.

Secondly, be careful when matching beers with desserts. It's a revelation for most people that beers go with sweet desserts at all, but in fact they're usually better partners than a sweet sauterne. However, do ensure that the beer is sweeter than the dish; otherwise the pairing becomes disharmonious.

Beyond that, the fun of beer and food matching is finding out what *you* think works. Here are a few tried and tested guidelines that work for most people:

PERFECT PARTNERS

Barley wine

These strong sipping beers are perfect with cheese and seasonal favourites such as a Christmas pudding.

Belgian *dubbel* and *tripel*

These are big, strong, usually sweet beers which require robust companions. Try dark roasts, stew and game.

Brown ale

A perfect partner for most meats. The beer's malt-driven sweetness harmonises with most meat dishes, especially those with some spice, such as a chilli con carne.

Fruit beer

Fruit beers work well with chocolate dessert but tend to be overwhelmed by fruit dishes. Sour fruit beers often pair well with goat's cheese or pickled fish such as gravlax.

India Pale Ale

Big, bold, US-style IPAs with lots of hops need foodie partners which are equally self-assured. Strong cheeses and Mexican-style spicy food are good, as are spare ribs with a spicy sauce. Less audacious English-style IPAs pair well with strong cheese and steak casseroles.

Lager and Pilsner

The soft delicate flavours of Pilsner-style beers partner well with shellfish, Asian spices, Thai dishes and Spanish tapas. Sweeter lagers work well with hotter curries.

Porter and stout

These dark beers work surprisingly well with desserts, and are marvellous with ice cream. They pair very well with blue cheeses such as Stilton. A traditional pairing is with oysters.

Pale ale and bitter

The perfect partner to English cheeses and traditional pub food such as steak-and-ale pies and sausages.

Weissbier

The banana and clove characteristics of a German-style wheat beer go well with a wide variety of foods including pasta, soft cheeses and loads of fish dishes.

Beer Genie

A licensee's view of beer and food matching

'We're the last pub in Essex,' says Mitch Adams, the owner of the Thatchers Arms in deeply rural Mount Bures. 'We're right on the county border and anyone driving by will soon be in Suffolk.'

In the last few years Mitch has been on a journey of a different kind. He's been organising highly successful, till-ringing beer and food matching evenings.

When Mitch took on the pub in 2007 he had to work hard to get people through the door. But his hard work has paid off. 'The village is quite small and spread out, with just 100 chimney pots,' says Mitch. 'We're a cross between a food-led pub and a community pub. I hate the word gastro!' He's proud that most of the food is sourced locally, which is important in a rural farming community.

His beer epiphany began while he was working for pub company Mitchells and Butler in London. 'I started to get into my beers, especially Belgian. Then I was invited on a beer and food matching evening at another pub. It was fantastic. I'd never been to anything like it before.'

From that point on he started to read and learn more about beers and food matching, leading him to have the courage and knowledge to put on a beery event at the Thatchers. 'At the first one, 18 people turned up. It was done while we were putting on a beer festival. People knew what our food was like and I think they were willing to embrace it. There were several women who came,

▼ Food and beer matching is not an exact science, but it is a lot of fun. (Beer Genie)

▲ Licensee Mitch Adams, standing rear left, delights in running beer and food evenings at his pub. (Beer Genie)

▼ A well-served and carefully chosen glass of beer is the perfect partner to many dishes. (Beautiful Beer)

they bought a wine in the bar before they came in, saying they didn't like beer and they were going to give the beer to their husbands. But they really enjoyed it and now they come into the bar and buy a beer and they talk about it too. It's great to see people choosing different beers to go with the courses of the meal.' At his latest beer and food evening more than 60 people were jammed into the bar.

So how should people go about choosing a beer and food matching? Mitch says: 'Remember to match the dominant flavour with the beer – this isn't always the main component of the dish. While seared scallops pair well with porters and stouts, when served with asparagus a better match would be a Belgian *tripel*. When planning a tasting evening try to keep lighter and weaker beers towards the earlier part of the menu, with stronger and darker beers near the end – a classic Czech Pilsner with a fried calamari or prawns building to a strong IPA (6 or 7%) with a curry, followed by a stout with cheesecake or barley wine with treacle tart.'

He recommends it's best to pair strong tasting foods with stronger beer. Spicy foods go well with strong IPAs and strong blue cheeses go well with Imperial stouts.

'Research your matches. Whilst it's not an exact science, a healthy understanding of the subject will make for a more convincing menu. And don't be afraid to ask other brewers what their favourite food matches are.'

The Thatchers Arms can be found at Mount Bures, Essex, CO8 5AT. Their website is at www.thatchersarms.co.uk.

◀ With some training, even the most daunting brewing set-up becomes easy to comprehend.
(Cath Harries)

Going on a brewing course

So, your first beers were a success and were drinkable. But are your skills good enough to think about turning a kitchen hobby into a business? Well, yes, they could be, and you'd be in good company, but some training would help.

Running your own brewery is many people's idea of a perfect lifestyle. Working hard during the day and then sampling a glass or two of the suds in the evening. It's a career change that many folk have already decided on; and the fact that there are more than 1,000 people in the UK running their own commercial breweries and making the beers that they want to drink and sell shows that it can be done. For some it's a lifestyle choice. Others see it is as a pathway to riches. But whatever your aspiration, it takes planning and training to become a commercial brewer, because if you don't get it right the dream could become an expensive nightmare.

Brewlab in Sunderland is one of several organisations around the country where people can get hands-on experience of the realities of working in a brewery. The company's three-day course is ideal for people thinking about setting up their own microbrewery. Normally about 20 students, including many women, attend each of its regular courses. All of them could be at different stages of their brewing journey, but they all share a love of beer and the desire to learn more about the process. The topics covered include beer tasting, recipe formulation, business start-up advice, brewery visits, marketing and brewery design.

Day one begins with an overview of the brewing process, followed by brewery design and layout and more details on the ingredients, as well as looking at the contribution of water and yeast. The second day includes recipe formulation, fermentation, racking and beer conditioning. Importantly there are modules on marketing and publicity, tax, and profit and loss, since in most small breweries the brewer has to have hands-on experience of every aspect of the business. The modules are designed to show the harsh realities of life, and reinforce the message that just because you can make a good beer, it doesn't mean that people will come to buy it.

The final day includes trips to several nearby breweries and talking to brewers who've already completed Brewlab courses. There's also an optional fourth day spent at High House Farm brewery, where students can observe and assess the brewing process from start to finish.

The Brewlab app also has a useful ingredient calculation tool for professional brewers that enables them to generate recipes in the same way as large professional brewing companies.

In the evenings students usually undertake some essential research and sampling in some of Sunderland's finest pubs.

Brewlab can be found at Unit 1, West Quay Court, Sunderland Enterprise Park, Sunderland, Tyne and Wear, SR5 2TE. Their website is at www.brewlab.co.uk.

Hop to it: growing your own hops

Do you brew your own beer? Well, why not grow your own hops, too? It's not as hard as you might think to grow these tall, exotic-looking plants.

For a successful hop harvest the bines require long hours of daylight, and the best latitudes for growing them are between 35° and 55°, in both the northern and southern hemispheres. The closer you are to the poles or the Equator, the harder it is to grow hops.

Once you get going you find that hop plants are easy to grow, hard to kill, and come back year after year. They're also easy to propagate, so they're easy to share among the home-brewing community.

The hop plant *Humulus lupulus* is a tall-growing perennial that arises from an underground rootstock or rhizome. The bine grows rapidly, and during the height of the season can grow up to 100cm per day, finishing up at a height of 9–10m.

Beer Genie

Beer Genie

▲ **Commercial hop gardens require large and extensive fields strung with wire, up which the bines grow.** (Beer Genie)

Tall the plants might be, but the important parts are the small hop cones, which are found the on lateral shoots. Hop varieties get their properties or active principles from small yellowish glands at the base of the cone petals within the bracts or scales. The gland is covered by a waxy skin, within which lies all the unique bittering (alpha acids) and aromatic (oil) compounds. These glands are referred to as *lupulin.* Hop plants are pretty forgiving plants and can tolerate dry, sandy soil or even clay, but prefer a rich, moist soil and lots of daylight sunshine. Some people have even successfully grown them in wooden barrels or large pots.

Once the hop plants get going you'll need to find a way of trellising them. In commercial gardens hops are grown on tall vertical wires. This makes them easier for harvesting but may not be that practical in a garden. However, hops will happily grow up alongside a house or up a wooden pole, or follow a wire strung between two buildings.

A few weeks after planting the root, hop shoots will emerge and will start hunting around for something to climb. If your trellis strings or hop poles are already in place, the shoots will often find them by themselves. If not you can help them by gently twisting the vines around the support. But remember, hops grow clockwise, so train them in that direction and the small spines on the shoots will help them grab and take hold. Beyond this hops don't require much care, though watering them in the morning is a good idea. However, hops can be plagued by aphids and spider mites, so it's important to watch out for these.

◀ **Hop bines often have to be persuaded to climb up their support.** (Beer Genie)

▼ **Hop expert Dr. Peter Darby, left, and Kent brewer Shepherd Neame's head of production, David Holes, are working to preserve old and threatened hop varieties.** (Shepherd Neame)

▲ **The annual hop harvest is a time of intense and hard physical activity for the workers.** (Tim Hampson)

▲ **Once the tall bines are cut, they are passed into a machine which cuts off the cones.** (Tim Hampson)

▲ **Once stripped, the cones are inspected by hand to ensure they are suitable for drying.** (Tim Hampson)

Between the end of August and the middle of September the hops should be ready to harvest. Ready-to-pick hops are aromatic and feel slightly dry and springy to the touch. Ideally you need to pick them before they start to turn brown. The best way to pick hops is when they're on the ground. Cut the string or pull out and lower the pole, then carefully pull off the small hop cones growing at the end of the tendrils.

Once the hop cones have been picked, the bines should be cut off about a metre from the ground. Then allow the bines to die back. After the first frosts, cut the hop bine to about 10cm from the crown. Feed it generously with compost or well-rotted manure to renew its mulch and it'll come back next year.

Commercially, hops are normally dried before use, but some brewers like to use their hops green. The flavours in freshly picked hops are very different from those in dried hops: the grassy, delicate citrus notes in fresh hops turn pungent and intense when they're dried. However, timing is crucial when brewing a green-hopped beer. The hops need to get from bine to the brewery quickly, otherwise all the delicate flavours will oxidise and disappear. Ideally the freshly picked hops need to be added into the copper within hours of picking. It can be a pressurised business.

It's possible to dry your own hops at home. A food dryer can help, or anywhere which is warm, dry and has good airflow. However, if you dry them it needs to be done quickly as you want to avoid them getting mouldy or going brown.

One or two plants are plenty for growing at home. You'll probably be surprised that despite the height and vigour of the bine, each plant will probably only yield a few grams of hops in its first year of harvest, though this should be more than enough to add to a brew. Depending on the variety, hops typically fully mature by the third harvest, and once established subsequent harvests should yield at least one kilogram of aromatic cones.

Hop plants are available from garden centres, and some home-brew suppliers will source them.

▼ **The majority of hops will be dried before they are ready for the brewers to weave their magic.** (Tim Hampson)

CHAPTER 4
THE BREWING PROCESS

The brewing process in a commercial brewery

Beer is a natural drink usually made from fermented cereals. The brewer extracts the sugar from the grain using hot water. Hops are added and the liquid is boiled. It is then cooled, yeast is added, and the fermentation process begins. Once the yeast has finished its magical work, converting the sugar into carbon dioxide and alcohol, we have beer. Well, nearly.

The beer is now allowed to condition, or mature, before it's put into a cask, keg, bottle or can. Some beers are clarified, others are served unfiltered. Some are pasteurised and others aren't. But one thing is certain – they're all beers.

It's such a simple process:

■ Malted barley is soaked in hot water to release the fermentable sugars.

■ The sugar solution is boiled with hops. This adds aroma and bitterness, and helps clarify the liquid and kill off any bugs in it.

■ The solution is cooled and yeast is added to begin fermentation.

■ The yeast ferments the sugars, releasing carbon dioxide and ethyl alcohol.

■ When the main fermentation is complete, the beer is bottled with a little bit of added sugar to provide the carbonation.

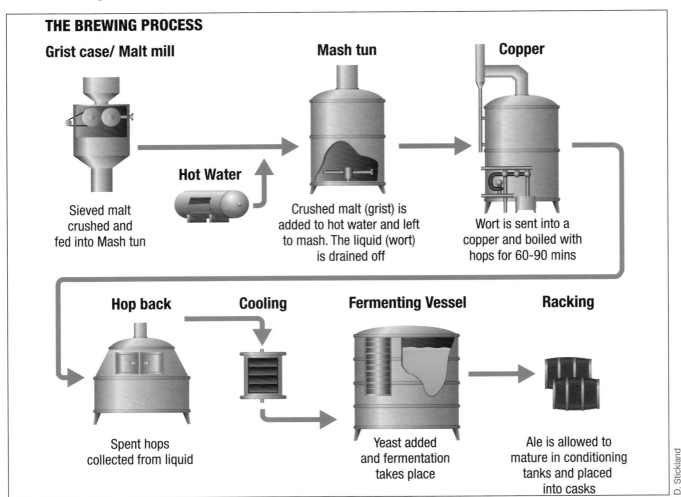

THE BREWING PROCESS

Grist case/ Malt mill

Sieved malt crushed and fed into Mash tun

Hot Water

Mash tun

Crushed malt (grist) is added to hot water and left to mash. The liquid (wort) is drained off

Copper

Wort is sent into a copper and boiled with hops for 60-90 mins

Hop back

Spent hops collected from liquid

Cooling

Fermenting Vessel

Yeast added and fermentation takes place

Racking

Ale is allowed to mature in conditioning tanks and placed into casks

D. Stickland

IN THE BREWERY – THE SEVEN STEPS FROM GRAIN TO GLASS

1 Whole malted barley and other grains are ground in a mill. The cracked grain is known as grist. Some brewers call this the grain bill.

a The grain usually arrives in the brewery as whole malted grains. (Tim Hampson)

b Once the required amount of malt for the brew has been weighed, it is poured into the grist mill. (Cath Harries)

c Grist mills come in many shapes and sizes, some are new, but most are old and quite noisy machines. (Cath Harries)

d Brewers hate wasting anything, and after the grist has been mashed it is collected and used as animal feed. (Cath Harries)

2

The grist is then mixed with hot water in a vessel known as a mash tun, to produce a sweet-smelling mash. This porridge-like mash is then left to stand. The heat of the water activates the enzymes in the malt so that they can break down the starch to fermentable sugars. This produces a sweet-smelling and tasting liquid. This is known as a single-infusion mashing. Some brewers run off some of the liquid into another vessel, heat it to a higher temperature and put it back into the tun, once, twice or even three times. This is known as single, double or triple decoction mashing. The higher temperatures draw out sweeter, more complex sugars from the malt.

a Harveys mash tun is essentially like a giant teapot, used to extract the goodness from grains rather than tea leaves. (Cath Harries)

b The temperature of the mash is critical, so brewer Miles Jenner regularly checks it. (Cath Harries)

c Once the optimum temperature has been reached, the mash is left to stand. This is when brewers have their breakfast! (Cath Harries)

d The liquid is drained through the bed of grains, which are then sparged with a fine spray of hot water to draw out even more fermentable sugar. (Cath Harries)

3 At the end of mashing, the sugar-rich, sweet wort is either strained though the bottom of the mash, or everything passes into a lauter, a large sieve. As the sweet wort runs off, the grain in sparged (rinsed) with more hot water to release the final sugars from the malt. The spent grain is used for animal feed.

a   The spent grain creates a thick porridge-like crust at the bottom of the mash tun. (Cath Harries)

b   In some modern breweries the spent grains are removed automatically. (Cath Harries)

c   However, in some breweries, such as Hook Norton, the mash tun has to be dug out manually. It's hard work. (Cath Harries)

d   Cleanliness is king in a brewery. Here a copper is being cleaned prior to use. (Cath Harries)

e   Spent grains are collected outside the Hook Norton brewery, to be used later for animal feed. (Cath Harries)

a · **The Rochefort brewing hall is beautifully elegant.** (Tim Hampson)

b · **The Pilsner Urquell coppers are powerfully graceful.**
(Tim Hampson)

c · **Once-busy coppers make grand centrepieces for a brewing museum.** (Tim Hampson)

d · **The Budvar coppers exude a quiet confidence.** (Tim Hampson)

e · **Hall & Woodhouse's former coppers are included in a visitors' tour of the brewery.** (Tim Hampson)

f · **Working coppers make a fine centrepiece to Meantime's bar and restaurant in Greenwich, London.** (Cath Harries)

4 The wort now passes into a brew kettle, sometimes known as a copper. The temperature of the water is bought up to boiling point. Hops are added at different times in the process – they add aroma and bitterness to the liquid and will inhibit the activity of unwanted bacteria. The boiling sterilises the liquid and stops all enzyme activity. Some brewers add other herbs and spices at this stage. At the end of the boil the spent hops are removed, sometimes by passing through a separate vessel called a whirlpool or a hopback. The spent hops are much sought after as a fertiliser.

g   Today, in many breweries copper has been replaced by stainless steel, as at the Krombacher brewery in Germany. (Tim Hampson)

h   Copper or steel, large or small, most kettles have some form of lid, or inspection panel. (Tim Hampson)

i   Prior to use, the hops required must be weighed. (Cath Harries)

j   Hops are added to the boiling wort. (Cath Harries)

k   The wort starts to bubble and foam as soon as it comes into contact with the hot water. (Cath Harries)

l   Sometimes the hops need a good stir. (Cath Harries)

m   It is important to check on the progress of the wort. (Cath Harries)

5 The wort is next cooled by passing through a heat exchanger, and is then put into a fermenting vessel. If it's too warm the yeast will die, too cold and the yeast will take a long time to do its work. The yeast is pitched (put) into the wort, and then the real magic of brewing begins, as yeast – as part of its lifecycle – produces carbon dioxide and alcohol from the sugar and millions more yeast cells.

a A heat exchanger is vital to get the unfermented wort down to the right temperature, ready for fermentation. (Cath Harries)

b Yeast might not look much, but without its lifecycle we wouldn't have beer or bread. (Cath Harries)

c In many breweries, beer is fermented in closed conical-shaped vessels. (Cath Harries)

d Fermenters are open vessels in many breweries. (Cath Harries)

e In open fermenters, once the yeast starts its work, a foaming head starts to form on top of the liquid. (Cath Harries)

f Rousing the liquid ensures efficient fermentation and viable yeast. (Cath Harries)

g Many breweries use strange-looking devices for collecting over-active yeast heads. (Cath Harries)

6 Once fermentation is finished the liquid is known as 'green beer' and it is removed from the yeast and given time to condition and mature. (Some of the yeast can be used for another fermentation, while excess yeast is often used as a health food.) During this time a secondary fermentation will take place and the flavours of the beer will develop. The beer is then put into a bottle, can, keg or cask.

a Keeping a record of every brew is very important. (Cath Harries)

b Once the beer has had its primary fermentation, it needs to be matured. (Cath Harries)

c Lagered beers are often kept at 0°C temperatures in caves deep underground for many days. (Cath Harries)

d Cask ale needs to be racked into barrels before it is sent out to pubs. It is often a manual process. (Cath Harries)

e Some breweries use a degree of automation to help staff rack beer. (Cath Harries)

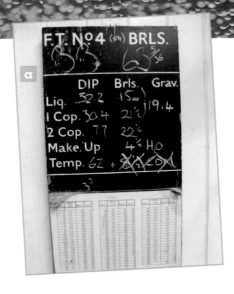

f   At the Cantillon brewery, in Brussels, beer conditions for many months in wooden barrels. (Cath Harries)

g   Care of beer in a pub's cellar is vital. A wooden peg (tut) needs to be driven into the barrel's shive to allow the living beer to breathe. (Cath Harries)

h   Before serving, a tap must be tapped/driven through the barrel's keystone. (Cath Harries)

7 Enjoy.

a   It is important to check the quality of the beer prior to serving. (Cath Harries)

b   A perfect pint, what could be better? (Cask Marque)

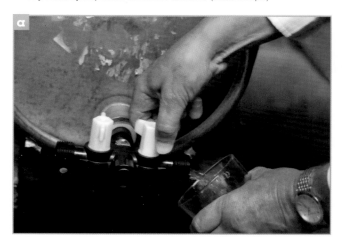

Home brewing

Making beer isn't difficult, but it takes time, and there will be moments when you'll be tearing your hair out. From culturing the yeast and starting to heat the water for the mash it can take weeks, or even months, for a beer to be ready to drink. And while good things do come to those who wait, patience isn't just a virtue – it's a necessity when waiting to try a new recipe or an experimental brew. But if all goes well the reward will be that marvellous moment when you take a first sip of a beer and discover that, yes, the effort, the hard work and the wait were all worth it.

But even the best-laid plans don't always work out. You might have the best equipment that money can buy, a recipe that's been meticulously followed, and equipment clean enough to have been used in a hospital operating theatre, but sometimes things can still go wrong. It will happen, but the chances are that there will be a fellow home brewer close at hand whose experience you can draw on. The best advice for the beginning home brewer is 'keep it simple'.

There's a wealth of experience for all home brewers to draw on – on the Internet, at home brew clubs or from home brew suppliers. Beer might be made from four simple raw materials – water, malt, hops and yeast – but there are so many variables. And like a mad juggler, the best brewers learn to recognise the variables and work with them. This is why brewing is an art, a craft and a science. When something goes wrong, it could be that the pH (acid/alkali) balance of the water wasn't right, or that the wort hadn't oxygenated enough, or

that something had changed in the malt or barley, or perhaps the yeast was put in too early. Each of these variables plays a part in how the beer turns out.

You'll be in good company – brewers at AB-In Bev, Carlsberg and Heineken all face the same challenges, albeit on a larger scale. However, it's unlikely that you'll want to turn out a mass-produced beer and want every pint that comes out of your fermenting vessel to taste the same as the last, and the one before that. With good practice most beers you produce will be drinkable and enjoyable. Of course things will go wrong, but don't be discouraged – being a home brewer takes time to perfect, and some say that that point is never reached. But the more you put in, the more you'll get out.

There are four different ways in which to brew your own beer:

1 Absolute beginner – using a starter all-in-one kit.
2 Malt extract plus addition of hops.
3 Partial mash/mini mash – malt extract, plus addition of malt, grains and hops.
4 All grain – full mash plus hops.

▼ **Stores like the Home Brew Shop, in Aldershot, are great places to seek ingredients, equipment and advice. Never be afraid to ask.** (Cath Harries)

Health and safety

Compared with some hobbies home brewing is relatively benign, but as it involves the boiling and moving about of lots of liquid it pays to be sensible. However, don't do as one person did. Rob Neale of home-brew supplier Malt Miller told me the story of a man who wanted to avoid getting up early in the morning to get the water heated for his mash, so he decided to put a timer on his boiler and set it to switch on for 5:30am.

Well, the heater came on and the water got hotter and hotter, and by the time our wannabe brewer had got out of bed, come downstairs and opened the kitchen door, his 25 litres of boiling beer had completely filled the room with steam. The paper had peeled off the wall and the glue holding his kitchen cabinets together had come apart and they were ruined.

It proved to be an expensive brew, as he had to buy his wife a new kitchen.

Some tips

1 Be aware that carbon dioxide is a by-product of the fermentation process and you don't want to be breathing lots of it in. However, given the likely scale of most home-brew operations, a well-ventilated room should suffice.

2 Many people successfully ferment beer in a glass demijohn/carboy. However, be careful not to pour in liquid that's very hot, as the demijohn could break. Also, be aware when handling one that it could shatter. Plastic or metal containers are generally safer.

3 If you're putting beer into bottles be aware that they too can shatter. Shattering can happen if a brew hasn't been fully fermented before bottling. However, it's said that you haven't become a proper home brewer until you've cleaned beer off a ceiling.

4 Clean and sterilise your equipment, especially anything that's going to come into contact with the wort after it's been boiled. The cleaner everything is, the less likely the beer is to become contaminated by bacterial infection. It won't kill you, but the beer will probably taste awful.

5 Boil with care. The steam coming off your brew is hot stuff – it will be in excess of 100°C and will scald you if you're not careful. And be cautious when carrying vessels containing hot water or shifting hot liquid between vessels.

6 You might not want to get water on the floor of your kitchen or the room where you're brewing, but you will. Be sensible and careful that you don't slip on it.

7 Malt is pretty cheap, so only buy what you need rather than keeping big stores of it. If mice find it they'll love it for lunch.

8 Keep powdered malt in the freezer, open containers of malt in the fridge, and hops somewhere cool.

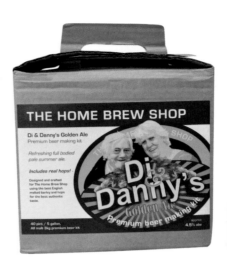

Cath Harris

BEGINNER: USING A STARTER KIT

This is the easiest and quickest method and you only need the barest essential equipment. There are plenty of kits around which come with all the equipment and ingredients to get going. If you can heat water and add it to a pot noodle then you can do this. Most kits produce acceptable beer.

A brewer's progress		
Method	**Need to buy**	**Equipment, technical expertise**
All-in-one kit.	A can of unfermented beer extract (hopped wort) – yeast is supplied.	Easy-peasy – no boiling – a good way to learn about fermentation and keeping equipment clean.
Extract + hops.	A can of malt extract – if you want you can choose the yeast and hops to be used or use those supplied with a kit.	Easy to do, but you must be able to boil wort for at least an hour. Brewer has more, if limited, control over flavour and style of the beer. A chiller or other means of quickly cooling the hopped wort before fermentation will make life much easier.
Extract + grain + hops.	Hop extract, grains and yeast.	Grains are steeped in hot water and removed, extract is added and boiled with hops. A muslin bag to hold the grain makes life easier, as does a larger copper. Choice of grains limited to crystal and roasted malts.
Extract plus – a partial mash.	As above, but with lots more choice of grain and malt.	Temperature control becomes more important, larger volumes of hot water are needed, grain will have to be sparged (rinsed with hot water). A good mash tun would help.
All grain.	No extract, just malt – approx 4–5kg needed for 20 litres + hops and yeast.	Greater control over the process is needed. But the brewer is in control of the recipe. A mash tun and the ability to sparge (rinse) the grain are needed.

MALT EXTRACT PLUS ADDITION OF HOPS

This method requires a bit more time, but it's worth it. It uses the same basic techniques as all-in-one kits, but you prepare the unfermented wort using water, malt extract (there are lots to choose from) and hops, now some craft is being added to the process. Some companies sell malt extract together with the correct hops to make a particular beer. The extract is dissolved in the water and then it's boiled for about an hour – the hops are added during this period – before cooling. Then yeast is added. There's a huge range of hops which all have their own unique flavours, aromas and levels of bitterness, which can be put into the boil or even added later.

Cath Harris

EXTRACT AND EXTRACT PLUS: PARTIAL MASH/MINI MASH

The process is almost the same as malt extract brewing, but it involves a new process – the steeping (soaking) of some malt or grain prior to the wort being boiled and the hops added. It's a way of adding extra body, flavours and colours to the finished beer.

The process isn't difficult but it takes some additional time, and you need to have an understanding of the flavours and characters of the different malts – those that can be steeped against those that need to be mashed. Steeping is ideal for extracting colour and flavours from caramel, chocolate and roasted malt.

The additional ingredients will be steeped in the hot water, or liquor as brewers call it, at a temperature of about 66–77°C for at least 30 minutes – the time and temperature depends on the recipe. Steeping or soaking speciality grain or crushed malt in the wort is like making tea, so don't try and rush it, as you want to get as much available flavour or colour out of it as you can. The bulk of sugars for fermentation come from the malt extract, so the temperature of the steeping isn't as critical as it would be for a full mash. It's best to put the ingredients for steeping inside one large muslin bag or several smaller ones. Steeping in bags makes handling the contents and emptying the saucepan much easier; without the bags a thick porridge-like substance will settle to the bottom of the pan.

As home brewers learn to master the process they learn how they can use different grains and extracts to create

Cath Harris

beers with a myriad different colours and styles. The home brewer may also experience sparging for the first time, if they pour hot water or hot wort over the bags of used grain to extract even more goodness from them. Most home brewers can produce world-class beers using this technique and happily stick with it and don't go on to all grain/full mash brewing.

ALL GRAIN/FULL MASH

This process follows the same principles as a mini mash, but you use malted, crushed grain (which you might have crushed yourself) instead of an extract. The malt, hops and yeasts you choose depends on the type of brew you want to create. The process followed is the same as in a commercial brewery. Now you'll have to sparge the grain, which means that you'll wash it with hot water to draw more of its essential fermentable sugars from it.

It's the most complicated of the brewing methods, needs the most equipment, takes the longest time to produce and needs careful temperature control. Once the mashing and sparging is completed the wort will be cooled and fermented. You'll have to get used to dealing with larger volumes of liquid than other procedures. It isn't ideal for a beginner, but it can be done. The process gives the brewer the greatest amount of freedom, flexibility and creativity.

Cath Harris

Getting started

Brewing at home is easy. Most of the equipment needed for a first brew will be found in a normal kitchen – a cooker, running water, some pans and some spoons will do for starters – but it's much easier with the addition of some extra bits and pieces that can easily be bought from a local home brew supplier or on the Internet.

THINGS YOU'LL NEED FOR A FIRST BREW

- Starter all-in-one home brew kit.
- A pot that will hold up to 20 litres of water – an 8-litre pot will be fine for smaller brews.
- A large spoon for stirring – it can be made from metal, wood or plastic.
- A can opener.
- A strainer.
- A measuring cup or jug.
- A small bowl or cup for mixing up the yeast.
- A place to ferment the beer. An even temperature is essential for fermenting beer. Ale-type beers might be fermented in an airing cupboard or a warm kitchen. Lagers might be better off fermenting and conditioning in a cooler place like a garage or shed.

Tips for a successful brew

Make sure all the equipment is thoroughly cleaned, preferably with a good disinfectant.

- Be patient, try to leave the beer to mature for as long as the recipe says – this will help improve its quality.
- Pour the beer carefully – this helps ensure that the yeast deposit stays in the bottle or cask.

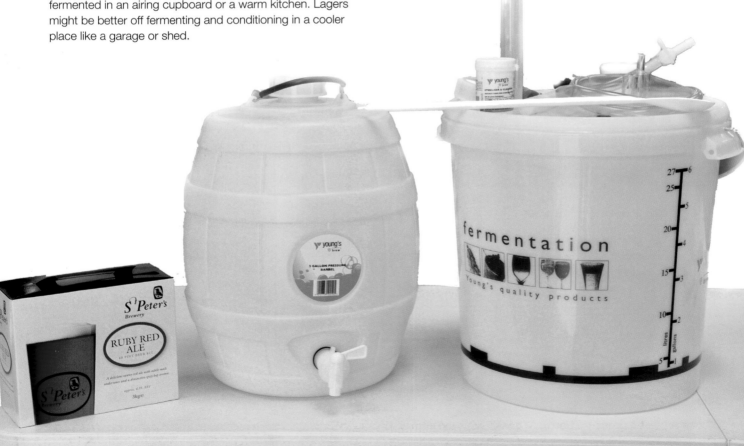

THINGS YOU'LL NEED TO GET

Many starter home brewing kits contain the basics necessary for your first brews. But you'll need to have:

■ **A fermenter:** This should be capable of comfortably holding 20 litres and a tight-fitting lid. Ideally the lid will have a hole into which an airlock can be fitted. However, many brewers use a glass carboy/demijohn – if that includes you, be careful how you pour hot liquid into it.

■ **Airlock and stopper:** Air is the enemy of all brewers, and the airlock allows the carbon dioxide created during fermentation to escape while keeping other air out.

■ **Thermometer:** Early brewers brewed by instinct and by testing the temperature of boiling liquid by sticking a finger into it! These days we're a bit more sophisticated and use a thermometer.

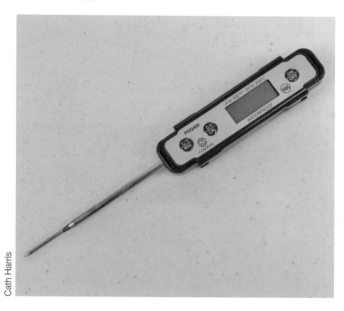

Cath Harris

■ **Hydrometer:** An understanding of some science will go a long way towards your becoming a successful brewer. A hydrometer allows the brewer to find the specific gravity of a beer (this is a measure of the sugar in the solution). A measurement is normally taken before and after fermentation and enables the brewer to determine the alcoholic content of the beer.

■ **Tubing:** Plastic tubing is necessary to transfer the beer between containers and eventually into a cask or a bottle – a process which in a brewery is called racking.

■ **A plastic pressure barrel or cask,** with a tap from which the beer can be poured into a glass. If the beer is being bottled, bottles, caps and a cap fixer are all necessary.

■ **Disinfectant:** The brewing equipment and area around it can never be clean enough. All equipment should be sterilised before use. And never be afraid to give surfaces a wipe down with a sterilising solution while you're brewing. Starter home brew kits will normally come with a supply of it, but excellent proprietary brands such as VWP Cleaner and Star San are available from home brew suppliers.

HOME BREW KITS

Most home brewers start off with an all-in-one home brew kit. These are very easy to use and only a little more complicated than pouring hot water into dried soup. They're a great first step into the world of brewing. Typically a kit will comprise a large can full of a treacle-like liquid containing an extract of malt and hops.

To make the extract much of the hard work has already been done by the kit manufacturer. The malt has been mashed in warm water to release the sugars, and then boiled with the hops to add bitterness and aroma. However, the brewing process is stopped before the yeast is added; instead the sweet wort is reduced to a sugary concentrate.

The home brewer dilutes the extract with some heated water in a fermentation vessel (which is actually supplied with some kits, though a clean plastic dustbin could be used). Some sugar might have to be added at his stage. Yeast is then added, and it's left somewhere to ferment for five to seven days – it might be longer if it's a lager or if the ambient temperature is low. During this period the yeast converts the sugars present into alcohol and carbon dioxide.

When the fermentation is over, no more bubbles will be seen to be coming from the liquid, and it's ready to go into a barrel or bottles.

Normally a little more sugar will be added and it'll be left for a couple of weeks to clear and mature. Some kits say that the beer can be fermented inside the barrel from which it's going to be poured. However, though beer was probably made in a single vessel in the very early days of brewing, if beer sits on dead yeast for any period of time it's likely to pick up some 'off' flavours.

The whole process from opening the kit to drinking an English-style ale will normally take about three weeks. A lager or a stronger beer might take a little longer. The resulting beer should be drinkable, and even if it doesn't taste quite as good as you hoped there's nothing in beer that's going to cause you food poisoning.

Brewing kits are an ideal way to begin to understand the brewing process and the logistics of home brewing; but as soon as you want to control and decide the colour, alcoholic strength and bitterness of the beer the limitations of kits quickly becomes apparent.

TYPICAL INSTRUCTIONS FOR MAKING A HOME BREW:

(All photographs by Cath Harries)

1 Read the instructions and familiarise yourself with the ingredients and equipment. All kits follow similar principles, but the details may vary.

2 Always thoroughly wash and sterilise all the equipment, even if it's brand new.

a Cleanliness is essential to good beer making.

b All the equipment which comes into contact with the beer needs to be sterilised.

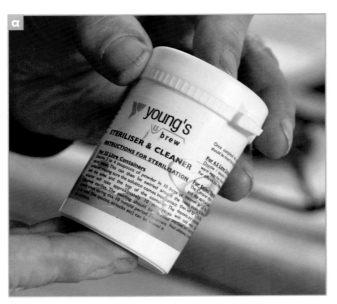

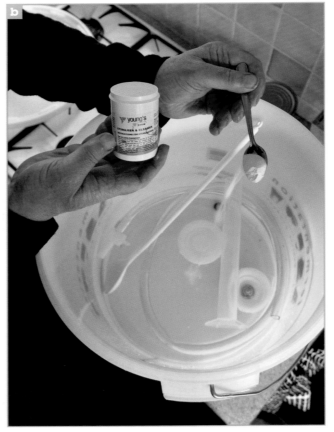

3 Open the beer kit can and warm in a bowl of water for at least five minutes to help soften and liquefy the contents.

a Pour some warm water from a kettle or tap into a bowl.

b Open the can with care – its contents are sticky and can get everywhere.

c Standing the cans in the bowl of warm water softens the treacle-like contents.

4 Pour the contents of the can into the fermentation vessel. Add boiling water as directed, fill the can with warm water and add it to the mix, and top up with cold water to desired volume. Some recipes might ask you to add dissolved or granulated sugar at this stage.

a Once softened, the contents of the can easily be poured into the fermentation vessel.

b Water can be boiled in a kettle or a saucepan, but remember, handle with care.

5 Thoroughly mix the contents together with the spoon.

6 Add the hops – these might just be in powder form. Then add the yeast as directed. If the yeast has to be cultured beforehand remember to use a sterilised container.

a Now's the time to add the hops. In this kit they come in a powdered form.

b Now add the yeast. Remember to carefully follow the instructions.

7 Let the beer ferment in a warmish place (probably between 18-20°C) as directed in the instructions. This could be anything from five to ten days. Fermentation will be complete when the bubbles stop rising.

a Close the fermentation vessel, fit the airlock and place the vessel where the temperature is suitable and stable.

b Once bubbles have stopped rising through the airlock, the beer is ready for the next stage.

8 Measure the specific gravity of the beer when the fermentation has finished.

a A simple hydrometer is very easy to use.

b It is important to get into a habit of making a note of the final gravity.

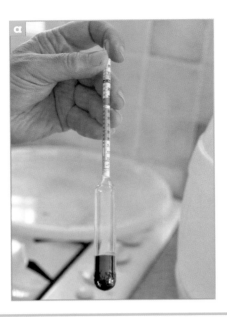

9 The beer should now be carefully siphoned into another fermentation vessel or cask and left to condition in a cool environment. A little sugar in liquid or granular form might have to be added equivalent to half a teaspoon per pint. This process could take anywhere between two and four weeks.

a Once fermentation is complete, carefully siphon off the beer.

b A gas canister fitted to the barrel helps to keep the beer fresher, and aids dispensing.

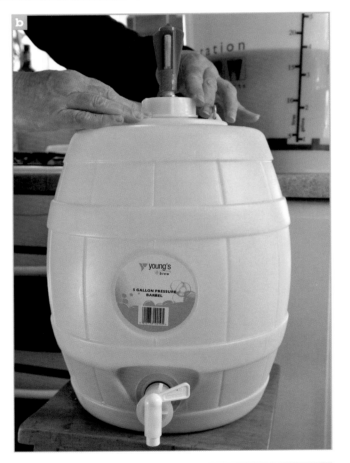

10 Siphon again into either bottles or a cask and add sugar for bottle fermentation.

11 Be patient and allow the beer to properly condition.

12 Invite your friends around and enjoy your very own brew.

MOVING ON: MALT EXTRACT

Some people are happy to stay brewing with all-in-one kits. However, they're missing out on so much, and those who wish to be more creative will soon want to move on. Brewing using malt extract is normally the next step on the journey for the home brewer. Malt extract is exactly what it says on the can – an extract of malt; the mashing has already happened. Many home brewer suppliers sell malt extract with specific hops to make particular beers.

The home brewer will dilute the extract and bring it to the boil, and add in the hops at the appropriate time. The wort will then be cooled and the yeast added. Next the wort will be fermented and conditioned.

Once you're using malt extract it's still possible to brew beer using kitchenware. However, there's plenty of specialist equipment available to make the process more sophisticated and easier for the brewer, and many people decide to invest in a boiler – also known as a copper or a kettle – for boiling the hopped wort.

Hops come in different forms, such as whole leaf, pellet or oil. Getting the hops out of the copper can be a messy process, so life becomes easier if you have a sieve to capture the used hops. Others put the hops into a muslin bag before placing them into the wort.

Brewing a malt extract beer is another seven-stage process:

(All photographs by Cath Harries)

1 **Boiling:** Dissolve the malt extract according to the instructions and then heat the liquor to boiling point – but make sure it doesn't boil over. Depending on the recipe, now is the time to start adding in the hops. This will usually cause a flurry of hot bubbles. Some brewers choose to put the hops inside a muslin bag, which is suspended in the boiling wort, rather than throwing them in directly. However, while being a lot less messy, there are those who argue that allowing the hops to move freely in the boiling wort is better at extracting bitterness and aroma from them. Boiling the wort sterilises it and causes an important chemical process called isomerisation to take place, which will help clear the beer. Isomerisation is actually the process of restructuring the hop oil so that it dissolves in water. The boiling does help to clear the wort, but that's through the coagulation of protein which is aided by copper finings. Expert brewers will check the pH of the wort, which optimally should be 5.2. They'll add in a little bit of lactic acid if necessary. Usually as soon as the boil is finished the hop bag is removed or the unfermented wort is drained off. If additional grains and malt were to be added to the liquor, this would have happened before the extract was put in.

a A good stainless steel boiler, especially if it has a tap, can make life easier.

b There are hundreds of different malt extracts to choose from.

c You can now choose the hops you want to use.

d Life can be easier if the hops are put into a linen bag.

e The bag needs to be immersed in the wort.

f Once the process is finished, the bag can be easily taken out and disposed of.

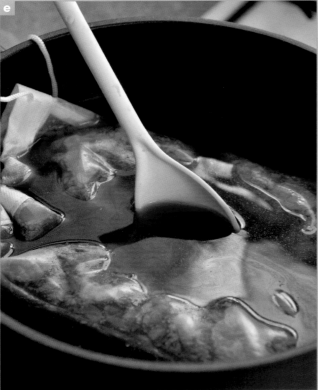

2 Cooling the wort: It's important to cool boiling wort to about 28°C as quickly as possible – anything higher will kill the yeast when it's added. The longer you take to do this the higher the risk of infection. Some cool the wort by immersing the boiler in a sink of cold water. However, this isn't that efficient a process, and involves the danger of moving vessels full of very hot liquid. Coolers can be built into the copper, or the wort can be run out and passed through a heat exchanger, which is attached to a cold water tap. There are also temporary coolers that can be put inside the boiler; these are often called 'spiral immersion wort chillers'. When the wort has cooled to 20°C, take a sample of the wort and, with your hydrometer, measure its original gravity. Keep a record of the density and the date of measuring.

a Knowing the temperature of the wort is important. Some vessels have built in thermometers.

b A heat exchanger is an efficient and safe way of cooling the wort.

c Many brewers use spiral immersion wort chillers.

3 Preparing the yeast: While the unfermented wort is cooling the yeast can be prepared, though some yeast will have to be prepared earlier. Each yeast is different and brings different characteristics to the beer. For most recipes it's important to create a yeast starter, as you'll want fermentation to begin quickly once the yeast is put into the wort. However, some yeasts are ready to go, with no prior preparation required. All brew shops have a range of brewing yeasts, which are available in liquid or powder forms.

4 Adding yeast and fermentation: Once the wort has cooled it can be siphoned off into the fermenting vessel. The yeast starter can now be added – brewers call this 'pitching the yeast'. You must ensure that it's thoroughly mixed throughout the wort. Initial fermentation can be quite vigorous and active, so be prepared for a large bubbly yeast head to form which might even overflow the vessel if an open fermenter is being used, or come out through the airlock.

5 Checking fermentation: For the next few days the fermentation must be watched – well, not for every minute of it, but it's important to keep a close eye on the temperature and ensure that it doesn't drop too much at night. After about seven to ten days the fermentation will stop. Another reading of the gravity of the liquid should be taken using the hydrometer (the original gravity is only ever taken once, hence original). Comparison of this figure with the OG taken allows the brewer to work out the strength of the beer. The fermented wort can now be run off into another vessel for conditioning.

6 Conditioning: To bring out the best of a beer it needs to be conditioned in a cool place, between 9–11°C for an ale and 0–3°C for a lager. It's a process similar to resting cooked meat for a period after it's taken out of the oven. At this stage brewers call it 'green beer'. During this time, some unwanted flavours are naturally removed and the beer will become clearer, as any yeast present will settle to the bottom of the vessel. There's no set time for conditioning but a week to ten days is usual. Lager beers take longer, and commercially some beers – notably Budvar – condition for 100 days. The home brew recipes for many historic old ales call for long periods of conditioning that can run into months.

7 Packaging the beer: The beer can now be run off into bottles, cask or keg.

PREPARING A YEAST STARTER

To make a typical starter, 50gm of malt extract will be dissolved in 500ml water, and 5g of a yeast nutrient or some sugar will be added. This is boiled for at least five minutes and then poured into a sterile glass flask, which is closed with a wad of cotton wool and allowed to cool. When it's cooled the yeast is added, the mixture is aerated, and the container is

(All photographs by Cath Harries)

kept at 21–26°C for 12 hours. Aeration can be done by just shaking the bottle, though there are more sophisticated ways of doing this. The yeast will start to multiply, and you should be able to see bubbles forming on top of the liquid.

Easy extract brewing

EQUIPMENT NEEDED

The minimum equipment you'll need for your first brew:

- 20–30-litre saucepan.
- Large stirring spoon (non-wood).
- Ordinary table spoon.
- Measuring jug.
- Glass container, with top, to take 500ml of liquid.
- Fermenter (food-grade plastic bucket or glass demijohn/carboy).
- Airlock (get from home brew shop).
- Disinfectant.
- Thermometer.

PREPARATION (UP TO AN HOUR)

Assemble ingredients

Gather together the ingredients for the brew.

Boil water

You'll need about 5 litres of sterile water for a variety of small tasks. Start by boiling the water for about 10 minutes. Let it cool, and cover. Add the sterilant.

What to clean

	Clean	Sterilise
Saucepan	*	
Stirring spoon	*	
Teaspoon	*	*
Measuring jug	*	*
Glass container for yeast starter	*	*
Fermenter and lid	*	*
Airlock	*	*
Thermometer	*	*

The importance of the cleanliness of your brewing equipment can't be emphasised enough, and everything that comes in contact with the wort after boiling must be sterilised.

MAKING WORT (1½ HOURS)

Now the work of brewing really begins, making from the malt the sweet liquid called wort that will later be fermented with yeast.

Prepare the yeast

If using dried yeast, rehydrate it – some people skip this step, but the best results are obtained by doing it. Put one cup of warm pre-boiled water into your glass jar and stir in the yeast. Cover with plastic wrap and wait 15 minutes.

Preparing a yeast starter

To make a typical starter, 50gm of malt extract needs to be dissolved in 500ml water and 5g of a yeast nutrient or some sugar. This is boiled for at least five minutes and then poured into a sterile jar, which has a top on to exclude air. When it's cooled the yeast is added, and the mixture is aerated, shaken or stirred. Some brewers allow the yeast to propagate for 12 hours before they use it.

Boil the brew water (liquor)

In the saucepan bring 8 litres of water to the boil. Pour this water into the fermenter and leave it to cool.

Adding the malt extract

Now bring 12 litres of water to the boil and add in the extract. If doing a partial mash you'll need to steep the crushed malt or grain in the water before adding in the extract. If making an extract beer, turn off the heat source when the water in the saucepan is boiling, stir in the malt extract, and stir some more. It's important to ensure that all of the extract is dissolved. Once everything has dissolved, turn the heat on again and resume the boil as directed in the recipe, stirring all the time.

Adding the hops

If you're using un-hopped extract, put in the first (bittering) hop addition and begin timing the hour-long boil.

Watch out for the water boiling over

As the wort boils, be careful it doesn't boil over. At first it will froth quite violently, and the frothing will continue until the wort has gone through what's known as the 'hot break' stage. Keep a close eye on it to ensure it doesn't boil over, turning the heat down slightly if needed. Stir frequently.

Adding more hops (optional)

Depending on your recipe, more hops are likely to be added at different stages of the boil, the last being just before it finishes.

Stop the boil after one hour or as specified in the recipe.

COOLING THE WORT

After the boil the wort must be cooled as quickly as possible to yeast pitching temperature, 18–28°C. Cooling could be done by putting the saucepan into a sink of cold water, but using a heat exchanger is much easier.

FERMENTATION

Pitching the yeast

Pour the rehydrated yeast solution into the fermenting bucket.

Add cooled wort

Pour the cooled wort into the fermenting bucket. Pour so that it splashes into the container and churns with the yeast solution. The churning adds in oxygen, essential for the yeast cells to thrive. Normally oxygen is the enemy of beer, but this is the exception to the rule.

If hops were added to the wort, remove by either straining the liquid as you pour it into the fermenter, or take out the muslin bags containing the hops.

Fermenting

Put the lid on the fermenter if using a plastic bucket and insert the airlock. Put it somewhere it can be undisturbed at a constant temperature of 18–21°C for two weeks. A little warmer won't do too much harm, but above 28°C will taint the flavour.

Clean up

Remember to clean up all the equipment you've used.

Be patient

After 24 hours the brew should be bubbling away. It's likely to bubble steadily for four to six days. However, the activity will decrease as the yeast chomps its way through the sugar. You can leave the beer in the fermenter for two weeks, but it would be best to carefully siphon it into another plastic bucket with a lid, or a barrel where it can condition for one to two weeks.

A full mash

(All photographs by Cath Harries)

HAVE A MASHING TIME

So, you've mastered using malt extract, boiling the wort and adding in hops. Now it's time to start brewing like a real commercial brewer and do a full mash brew. It's a bit more complicated, and requires additional equipment, but if you've been adding extra malt and grains to the mash you're already halfway there with the process. The kitchen might be getting a little cramped, but the likelihood is you'll start to brew even better beers.

The additional part of the process is that instead of diluting a pre-prepared commercial extract of malt, you'll be making your own. You'll also be boiling and needing more hot water, and you'll have to find a way of getting as much as possible of the sweet goodness you need from the malt once the wort has been drained off. This process is known as sparging, and involves you passing hot water slowly through a bed of wet malt to rinse out the final residual sugars.

The advantage of doing your own mashing is that you'll have much more control over the beers you make. Instead of buying the malt extract from your brew shop, you're going to buy the malt and create the mix you want.

The malted grain usually comes ready milled, as this is easiest. Your supplier should supply the grain in sealed bags or containers, having ground it to the size that you want. Some brewers don't use a mash tun, but instead steep their grist in a muslin bag (sometimes known as a lauter bag).

So what's happening in the mash?

Some science, and why the 65–66°C temperature is important.

Malt comprises a number of different sugars called maltose and dextrins. The temperature of 65–66°C produces the best balance of maltose, which is a fermentable sugar, and dextrins and other complex unfermentable sugars, which add body to the beer. The nearer mash temperature is to 60°, the higher the proportion of maltose. This will result in a thinner beer with less body, as the dextrins supply much of the beer's flavour. The nearer the temperature is to 70°, the higher the proportion of dextrins, which is likely to lead to a thicker, more syrupy beer due to the higher proportion of unfermented sugar. Higher temperatures are often better for full-bodied stouts.

Typically the malt will sit in the water for an hour. This is the time when many commercial brewers break for their breakfast, but before they go they'll ensure that the water in the boiler is being heated to 78°C for the next stage of the process.

▼ Some brewers use a hand-powered mill to make their grist.

▼ Easy to use, a mill cracks grains to the correct size for mashing.

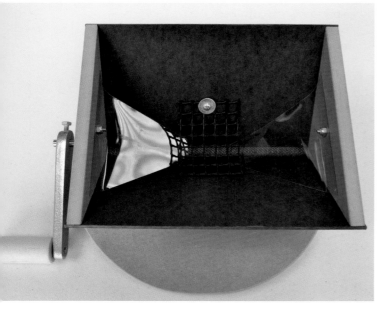

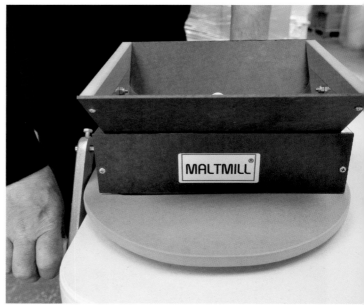

▲ ▼ **Putting the grist for mashing into a bag can make life much easier for the home brewer. It's best to devise a way of suspending the bag over water, as this will make it easier to remove and drain. This is important for large brews, when the grain bill is quite heavy.**

This normally requires a smaller size of milled grain.

As the brewer, you'll have to decide how much malt and what types you want for each beer. You'll then have to heat the liquor in your mash tun to a specific temperature and carefully add the malt. The temperature is key, as it's the temperature which decides how much of the sugar in the malt is extracted and what qualities it has.

However, wherever you're brewing, even if you're still in the kitchen, it helps if you arrange the equipment so that the wort flows – using gravity – through a mash tun, into which you've put the crushed malt, through a lauter tun (a fancy brewing word for a sieve) into the copper or kettle. Some brewers use a vessel that combines the attributes of a mash and lauter tun in one go. And the more resourceful will make the vessels out of adapted picnic coolers and other plastic vessels rather than buy bespoke units from a home brew supplier.

A successful and simple system for brewing 23 litres of beer could include the following:

◼ Something to boil the water in – this is your hot liquor tank.
◼ A combined mashing and lauter vessel, usually a pot of 19–24 litres with a sieve or filter at the bottom to keep the grains in, and a means of slowly pouring hot water over the grain. This could be a watering can or a more sophisticated rotating sparge arm.
◼ A copper cooling coil, such as a simple immersion chiller.
◼ A fermenting vessel.

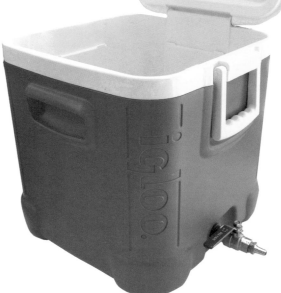

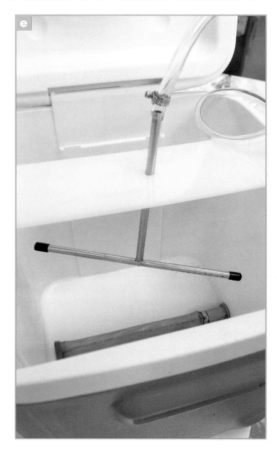

a Vessels like this can be used as a hot liquor tank, mash tun and a boiler/kettle.

b An integrated thermometer makes temperature control much easier.

c Inside a boiler. The heating elements can clearly be seen.

d Boilers come in many forms – this one is heated electrically.

e The sparge arm, which rotates as it pours water over the grain, fitted inside a mash tun made from a picnic cooler.

DOING THE MASH

The simplest mash is called a single infusion mash: the water is raised to one temperature and then the malt is put in. There are other more complicated infusions which involve raising the water's temperature up by a series of steps. Each different temperature in a stepped mash is held for a period of time, which draws out different attributes and characteristics from the malt.

Add the water to the mash tun. The water can either be pre-heated to 72°C or heated in the vessel. The milled grain is added in a slow controlled manner, and, once in, stirred continuously until properly wetted. Typically a brewer will use about 2.5 litres of water per kilo of malt.

The temperature will now drop to 65–66°C, and the brewer will need to maintain this temperature for 60 minutes, though a fall of one or two degrees won't be the end of the world.

While all of this is going on, heat the water that will be used for sparging. About 20 litres will be needed, heated to 76–78°C.

Top tips

- **Cleanliness – everything which comes in contact with the beer during the brewing process must be sterilised.**
- **Keep good records – the better the records you keep, the better your beers will be and the more likely you are to be able to recreate the perfect brew.**
- **Be prepared to learn from mistakes.**
- **Don't be afraid of a little science – the more you understand the raw materials and the processes, the better your beers will be.**
- **Talk to other brewers and share experiences.**

BOILING THE WORT

The hard work is almost over. Now it's time to boil the wort. The process from here on is exactly the same as if you had used malt extract. The wort is boiled, hops added, cooled, and then put into the fermenter.

Doing the sparge

Once mash has sat for its allotted time – normally 60 minutes – the wort is separated from the grain by draining it out of the bottom of the mashing vessel. The malt will have become a thick bed at the bottom of the vessel, and as the wort is drained away the hot water from your hot liquor tank will be poured slowly in from above, ideally at the same speed as the liquid is leaving the vessel. This is the process known as sparging, in which the rinsing of the grain extracts its remaining sugar.

Some brewers carefully pour the hot sparge water in using a jug, or even a watering can, but there are many commercial pieces of equipment available to do this, such as a rotating spare arm, through which the water passes.

The 78°C temperature of the sparge water lowers the viscosity of the sweet wort, thinning it down so that it flows better, allowing a good separation from the grain. Higher temperatures than this will result in the extraction of unwanted tannins and starch from the grains, causing harshness and haze problems.

If the sweet wort is cloudy, it can be carefully poured through the grain bed again, which will further help to filter it. The wort should be allowed to rest for about ten minutes, which helps stop unwanted flavour and aids clarification of the liquid.

As a rough guide, sparge until you have approximately 28 litres of wort in your boiler.

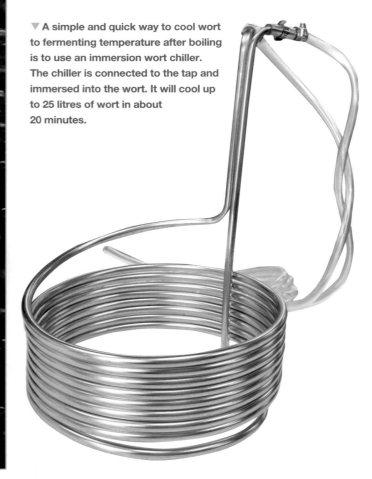

▼ A simple and quick way to cool wort to fermenting temperature after boiling is to use an immersion wort chiller. The chiller is connected to the tap and immersed into the wort. It will cool up to 25 litres of wort in about 20 minutes.

Cask, bottles or keg?

The next big step in your brewing journey is about to begin – you have to decide if you want to put your beer into a cask, bottle it, or to use a Cornelius keg.

(All photographs by Cath Harries)

BOTTLING

Equipment
- 48 (440ml) bottles.
- Bottle brush cleaner.
- Bottle capper.
- Bottle caps.
- Bottling bucket (basically another fermenter bucket with a spigot and bottle filler).
- Racking cane/siphon/bottle filler.
- Sugar (approximately 100gm).

What to clean

	Clean	Sterilise
Bottles	*	*
Bottle caps		*
All siphoning equipment	*	*

Prepare your bottles
A typical 20-litre batch requires 48 x 440ml brown bottles, thoroughly cleaned and sterilised. They can be dried on a bottle-drying tree or rack. The bottle caps and siphoning equipment must also be sterilised.

a Bottles need cleaning before use, especially if they have been used before.

b Bottle-drying trees make life much easier.

c Effective crown-capping is essential for good bottled beer.

d A hand-held crown-capper.

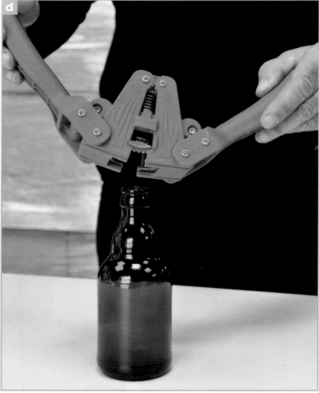

Prepare the priming sugar

Adding sugar to the beer will provide carbonation, the bubbles that will help it sparkle. Typically you'll need about 100gm brown sugar boiled in 600ml of water.

Add the beer to the priming sugar

Sterilise a plastic bucket similar in size to the fermenting vessel. Pour in the priming solution. Ensure the end of the siphon is under the beer so that it mixes with the primer without aerating it. If you don't have a second container, then the primer can be carefully added to the fermenting vessel. Allow the sediment to settle. Then, using the siphon, fill the bottles to about 2.5cm from the top.

Cap the bottles

Crimp the tops on to the bottles and store at room temperature for about two weeks.

Chill as required before serving. Open the beer, pour carefully to avoid disturbing the yeast sediment at the bottom, and enjoy.

PUTTING YOUR BEER INTO A BARREL

Barrels are good for English-style ales, or any beer that doesn't need masses of carbonation. They're easy to clean and sterilise and the beer can be put into one straight from the fermenter.

- Clean and sterilise your barrel.
- Dissolve 80g of sugar in some boiling water and allow to cool. Add this to the barrel.
- Carefully siphon the beer from the fermenter into the barrel. It's important not to aerate the beer, so be gentle. Close the top tightly.
- Leave the barrel at room temperature for a week to allow the priming sugar to do its work. This will create carbon dioxide and give the beer its natural fizz. Then move the barrel to somewhere dark and cool for storage – a garage or cellar is ideal.
- Some barrel systems allow for carbon dioxide to be injected into the beer to stop air coming into contact with the beer as it's drained off.

PUTTING YOUR BEER INTO A CORNELIUS KEG

The Cornelius keg (sometimes known as a corney or soda keg) is a pressurised container originally developed for serving soft drinks in pubs. They typically hold 19 litres of beer, so if you're doing a bigger brew the beer left over will need to be bottled. A keg can fit into a large fridge and doesn't need priming sugar, as carbon dioxide is used to dispense the beer. A small amount of carbon dioxide will have to be added at the time of filling, but other than that filling is the same as for a barrel.

Cornelius kegs have become regarded as the best way to dispense home-brewed beer, but you'll also need to have a CO_2 injection system and a dispensing tap.

Yeast

Yeast is all around us. Since ancient times brewers have known that some form of transformation took place to change wet grain into a life-enhancing drink, though they didn't understand the process. And all the while – unknown and, indeed, unseen – yeast was voraciously eating the sugar in primitive wort (unfermented beer) to convert it into carbon dioxide and alcohol.

SPONTANEOUS FERMENTATION

There was a time when all beer was made in this way. As the boiled wort cooled it became a suitable feeding ground for the yeasts that were in the air. From Asia to Africa and on to Latin America, porridge-like brews made with locally grown cereals, roots and saps were being transformed into a beer-like drink.

Living yeast leads a vigorous life. Swirling, moving, creating heat and a foaming head. This frantic activity is best seen a few days after the yeast has been pitched into the wort. It's not unusual for home brewers to deal with yeast heads overflowing on to the floor, and in days gone by the brewer

Cath Harries

would take some of this foamy head and pour it into the next brew, a process which, as we've seen, is known as 'pitching'.

The transference of the good yeast from brew to brew was an empirical but unintentional process of yeast selection. In England the brewers would simply say 'God is good', for they had no word for yeast and didn't know that they were transferring millions of vibrant yeast cells. It wasn't until the mid-19th century that the process became understood.

CHOOSING YEAST

Yeast selection is of prime importance to the home brewer. There's no point buying the finest malts and hops and then using yeast unsuitable for the style of beer you plan to create.

Yeast for home brewers generally comes in two types, liquid and dried. Dried yeasts are easy to use, cheap, and they have a much longer shelf life than liquid yeasts, but the choice of dried yeast strains is very limited in comparison to liquid, and some people say they don't have such a great depth of flavour.

Liquid yeasts require refrigeration, have a limited shelf life, and are more expensive. However, there's a huge range of them, which gives the home brewer great scope for experimenting, and although they're more expensive they can easily be reused by storing some of it from a primary fermentation in a sterilised jar in the fridge for a couple of weeks before using it again in a new fermentation. Yeast's characteristics are usually described in terms of taste profiles, such as fruity, dry or clean, and also by the level of flocculation and attenuation. Some Belgian and wheat beer yeasts have banana flavours, while clove flavours can be found in some German yeasts. Indeed, more than 500 flavours and aromas are derived from yeast, which is why the choice is important.

YEAST FLOCCULATION

Flocculation is the clumping together of yeast cells at the end of fermentation and how quickly they drop out of solution following fermentation. Yeast strains are separated into three main degrees of flocculation – high, medium, and low. An

English ale yeast is highly flocculent, and will quickly settle at the bottom of the fermentation tank. An example of a less flocculent strain would be a *hefeweizen* yeast.

Highly flocculent strains make beer that falls clear very soon after fermentation is over. With a less flocculent strain, you'd have to wait longer for the beer to clear. Highly flocculent yeasts are essential for English-style ales, which have a shortish conditioning time compared with lagered beers.

YEAST ATTENUATION

Attenuation is a measure of what percentage of the malt sugars the yeast consumes during fermentation. If the fermentation went to 1.000 gravity, that would be 100% attenuation. Understanding the different attenuation ranges of each strain will help determine the terminal gravity of the beer. This is calculated by subtracting the final gravity from the original gravity and dividing this result by the original gravity. For example, if you made an OG 1.060 ale and it finished at a gravity of 1.012, the apparent attenuation would be 80% – *ie* (60–12)/60 = 0.80. The higher the percentage, the higher final volume that's likely to be achieved from a given starting wort. But don't worry if you aren't good at maths; there's plenty of software on the Internet which will do all the calculations the home brewer needs.

▼ **Some yeasts are like children – they demand a lot of care and attention.** (Cath Harries)

▲ **Part of the fun of home brewing is learning about the characteristics of different yeasts.** (Cath Harries)

YEAST STRAINS

Home brew suppliers will be able to provide a yeast strain capable of producing just about every commercially available beer and every possible beer style, from English ales to Belgian *lambic*.

There are far too many yeast strains to list all of them here, and anyway, yeast suppliers are constantly updating their catalogues. However, when designing a beer it's important to understand the characteristics of different strains, as they can have a profound effect on the beer being made, as with this Wyeast strain:

Wyeast strain: 1007 German Ale

A true top-cropping yeast with low ester formation and a broad temperature range. Fermentation at higher temperatures may produce mild fruitiness. This powdery strain results in yeast that remains in suspension post-fermentation. Beers mature rapidly, even when cold fermentation is used. Low or no detectable diacetyl.

Attenuation:	73–77%.
Flocculation:	Low.
Temperature range:	13–20°C.
Alcohol tolerance:	Approximately 11% ABV.

It can be used for American wheat or rye, *Berliner weisse*, *biere de garde*, and *Kölsch* styles.

Wyeast strain: 1968 London ESB Ale

A very good cask-conditioned ale strain from the same company, this extremely flocculent yeast produces distinctly malty beers. Attenuation levels are typically less than most other yeast strains, which results in a slightly sweeter finish. Ales produced with this strain tend to be fruity, increasingly so with higher fermentation temperatures of 21–23°C. A thorough diacetyl rest, to stop unwanted butterscotch flavours forming, is recommended after fermentation is complete. This is likely to involve storing the beer at a specified temperature for a couple of days. Bright beers are easily achieved within days without any filtration.

Attenuation:	67–71%.
Flocculation:	Very high.
Temperature range:	18–22°C.
Alcohol tolerance:	9% ABV.

It can be used for many ales, IPAs and barley wines.

Whites WLP300 Hefeweizen Ale Yeast

This famous German yeast is a strain used in the production of traditional, authentic wheat beers. It produces the desired cloudy look and the banana and clove nose traditionally associated with German wheat beers.

Attenuation:	72–76%.
Flocculation:	Low.
Optimum fermentation temperature:	20–22°C.
Alcohol tolerance:	Medium.

Wyeast 2000 Budvar Lager

The Budvar strain has a nice malty nose with subtle fruit tones and a rich malt profile on the palate. It finishes malty but dry, well balanced and crisp. Hop character comes through in the finish.

Attenuation:	71–75%.
Flocculation:	Medium–high.
Temperature range:	9–13°C.
Alcohol tolerance:	8% ABV.

It can be used to make Bohemian Pilsner, American Pilsner, Dortmund export, and Lite American lager.

Whites WLP630 *Berliner Weisse* Blend

A blend of a traditional German *weizen* yeast and lactobacillus to create a subtle, tart, drinkable beer. Can take several months to develop tart character. Perfect for traditional *Berliner weisse*.

Attenuation:	73–80%.
Flocculation:	Medium.
Optimum fermentation temperature:	20–22°C.
Alcohol tolerance:	5–10%.

Whites WLP862 Cry Havoc

Licensed from US brewer Charlie Papazian, this strain can ferment at ale and lager temperatures, allowing brewers to produce diverse beer styles. The recipes in both of Papazian's books, *The Complete Joy of Homebrewing* and *The Homebrewer's Companion*, were originally developed and brewed with this yeast.

For ales:
Attenuation:	66–70%.
Flocculation:	Medium–low.
Optimum fermentation temperature:	20–23°C.
Optimum cellaring temperature:	10–13°C.

Alt beers can be cellared at lagering temperatures.

For lagers:
Attenuation:	66–70%.
Flocculation:	Low.
Optimum fermentation temperature:	13–14.5°C.
Optimum lagering temperature:	0–3°C.

Malt and grain

When it comes to designing and making a beer, the choice and mixture of malts used is crucial, for it's malt that gives beer its main flavour, colour, body, head retention and – importantly – alcohol.

When choosing a malt two crucial factors are its colour, which can go from light to dark, and its diastatic power – its potential to have the starch it contains broken down into even simpler fermentable sugars during mashing.

There's a scale for determining the colour of malt and beer, which is used throughout Europe. The colour is measured in EBC units, where the lowest rating is the palest colour. The very palest Pilsner malts could have an EBC of 2.5; the darkest are roasted barley and black malts, which could weigh in at 1500 EBC.

Diastatic power is normally shown as a percentage, and its strength is important, as if the brewer doesn't have sufficient diastatic enzymes in their mash there won't

Cath Harries

Cath Harries

be enough sugar, and the resultant beer is likely to be only partially fermented, very sweet, and will have an undesirably low alcohol level.

A common error made by partial mash brewers is to take several kilos of exciting-sounding speciality malts and try to use them without the addition of sufficient, or any, pale base malt. Only the palest malts contain the enzymes necessary for starch conversion, and in most circumstances the bulk of any beer recipe must consist of such malts. The diastatic power of each malt is often shown as the maximum percentage that's recommended in the grist.

The following section shows the likely colour of different malts and gives a guide to how much of it could be used in the mash – however, always check with your brewing supplier on the characteristics of malts, as they can vary.

MALTED BARLEYS

Acid malt

Contains lactic acid and helps reduce the pH of a brew, resulting in a beer with a softer palate. Lager brewers recommend its use.
Colour 3 EBC, maximum percentage 10%.

Amber malt – UK

Not widely used, this is an interesting alternative to crystal malt in bitters, and outstanding in dark ales, especially porters.
Colour 50–90 EBC, maximum percentage 20%.

Aromatic malt – Belgium

Aromatic malt provides a very strong malt flavour and aroma. Although not a roasted malt, it's kilned until the desired colour is obtained. Perfect for any beer in which a high malt profile is required.
Colour 150–160 EBC, maximum percentage 20%.

Belgian pale malt

Darker and more flavoursome than its British equivalent, this is a must-have malt for anyone wanting to produce Belgian-style ales.
Colour 7 EBC, maximum percentage 100%.

Belgian biscuit malt

Lightly roasted, it needs to be used sparingly. Gives a distinctive sweet biscuit character to a finished beer.
Colour 50 EBC, maximum percentage 15%.

Black malt

This is made by roasting British pale malt as far as possible without burning it. It's the preferred darkener in sweeter stouts and porters and can be used for minor colour adjustments in other beers.
Colour 1400 EBC, maximum percentage 10%.

British caramalt

The palest of all crystal malts, it introduces a crystal character without unduly darkening the beer. Particularly suitable for pale ales and bitters.
Colour 30–40 EBC, maximum percentage 20%.

Brown malt – UK

Brown malt can also add complexity to styles such as porter and old ale.
Colour 140–160 EBC, maximum percentage 20%.

Carahell

Its prime use is to accentuate the fullness of flavour of German festival beers, although it's unsurpassed as a flavour booster in low-strength lagers. It greatly increases head formation and retention.
Colour 20–30 EBC, maximum percentage 40% (higher in low alcohol beers).

Cara amber

A malt from Weyermann in Bamberg. It helps improve flavour stability and promotes fuller body. Provides a deep red colour. An interesting addition for all amber and dark beers.
Colour 60–80 EBC, maximum percentage 20%.

Carapils malt

Usually derived from German-grown Bavarian spring barley. The malt is ideal for use by extract brewers because of its sugar content.
Colour 3–5 EBC, maximum percentage 10%.

Caramunch – Germany

Although only used in small quantities, this has a marked effect on the fullness of flavour and aroma in golden to brown lager beers and ales.
Colour 80–100 EBC, maximum percentage 10%.

Cara red

A malt from Weyermann in Bamberg, Germany. It's used to add body and increase malt aroma in many beers. It helps create colours of great depth and a reddish hue.
Colour 40–60 EBC, maximum percentage 10%.

Chocolate malt – UK

A highly roasted malt which when used in small quantities imparts a rich chocolate and mocha coffee flavour to stouts and porters. It can be used to add some colour and a hint of taste to bitters.
Colour 800 EBC, maximum percentage 5%.

Crystal malt – UK

The powerhouse for many classic British beers. It adds sweetness, and adds balance to high hop rates. It can come in a wide range of colours.
Colour 80–140 EBC, maximum percentage 20%.

Dark crystal malt – UK

Excellent for use in beers that need a deep copper colour without lots of crystal character. It's useful when making porters and old ales.
Colour 230–250 EBC, maximum percentage 20%.

Diastatic amber malt – Belgium

A very pale, if not the palest, roasted malt, this is often used for Belgian and British-style beers.
Colour 50–60 EBC, maximum percentage 80%.

Lager malt

A British version of Pilsner malt, for which it can be substituted. The inclusion of acid malt is desirable if using it.
Colour 3 EBC, maximum percentage 100%.

Light chocolate malt

Needs to be used sparingly. It gives rich chocolate and even coffee flavours to brown ales, stouts and porters.
Colour 600 EBC, maximum percentage 5%.

Maris Otter pale malt

Light in colour, it's often used to produce light-bodied golden ales.
Colour 2.5 EBC, maximum percentage 100%.

Mild ale malts

Mild ale malt is kilned slightly hotter than pale malt to give a fuller flavour. Its luscious, thirst-quenching sweetness underscores the best mild ales.
Colour 6 EBC, maximum percentage 100%.

Munich malt

Munich malts provide the glorious notes that give beers from one of the world's greatest brewing cities their rich sweetness. It's often used in small quantities to add richness to other beers and is now widely used by many home brewers.
Colour 15–25 EBC, maximum percentage 100% (although rarely used at over 80%).

Pale crystal malt

A lighter version of the classic British crystal malt. It helps increase body and fullness while preserving a pale colour. Suitable for bitters and ales, it can add sweetness to a beer while helping balance high hop rates.
Colour 80–140 EBC, maximum percentage 20%.

Pale malt

The heart and soul of many traditional British ales. Maris Otter is favoured by many real ale brewers, but other varieties include Halcyon, Optic, Pearl and Golden Promise. Each is likely to behave slightly differently in the mash tun, and each brings a different nuance to the finished brew. The joy is finding out what each does.
Colour 4–5 EBC, maximum percentage 100%.

Pilsner malt

Probably the world's most widely used malt, it's usually produced from German, Belgian or Czech barley. Pilsner malt can be used on its own, provided the pH of the mash is correct, or in combination with other grains to produce the classic Continental lager beers. The inclusion of a small amount (3–5%) of acid malt is highly recommended when brewing Pilsners.
Colour 2.5 EBC, maximum percentage 100%.

Rauchmalz smoked

Any beer lover who's ever been to the magical medieval town of Bamberg in Germany has delighted in trying beers made with malts kilned over open fires made from beech wood logs. The phenols in the wood give the beer a smoky taste and aroma. It can be used in small quantities in many different beer styles, producing some interesting and intriguing flavours.
Colour 3–6 EBC, maximum percentage 100%.

Special B – Belgium

This malt is a cross between dark caramel malt and medium roasted malt. It provides distinctive characteristics to many Belgian-style beers. It's often used successfully in darker English ales.
Colour 250–300 EBC, maximum percentage 10%.

Vienna malt

Germany's Märzen and Oktoberfest beers, which are a golden colour and have full malt flavour, are reliant on this marvellous malt.
Colour 6–8 EBC, maximum percentage 100%.

OTHER MALTED GRAINS

Chocolate wheat malt

Roasted to a very high colour, it's primarily used for top-fermented ales such as *alt* and dark wheat beers. Even in very small quantities it intensifies the beer's aroma, as well as its colour.
Colour 800 EBC, maximum percentage 2%.

Crystal rye malt

Strongly flavoured and distinctive, this is becoming a favourite of many American home brewers. Use sparingly in dark beers or a bit more generously in German-style *roggenbiers*.
Colour 100–120 EBC, maximum percentage 10% (more for a strong rye flavour).

Crystal wheat malt

A crystal coloured malt that adds colour, intensity and wheat aromas to many top-fermented beers.
Colour 100–120 EBC, maximum percentage 15%.

Cath Harries

Dark wheat malt – Germany

Despite its name this is light in colour and has a lot more flavour than other wheat malts. It's used by home brewers making their own interpretation of an *alt*, *weissbier* or *Kölsch*. It can add flavour to lower-strength English ales.
Colour 15–17 EBC, maximum percentage 70%.

Malted oats – UK

Oats add a rich creaminess and a mellifluous mouth feel to a beer. Beware old recipes that call for large quantities to be used, as they're best used cautiously.
Colour 2 EBC, maximum percentage 5%.

Pale rye malt

When used sparingly rye adds some interesting and distinctive taste notes to ales. It can be used along with crystal and roasted rye malts to brew the classic German top-fermented rye beer *roggenbier*.
Colour 4–6 EBC, maximum percentage 50%.

Pale wheat malt

A favourite of many who make German-style top-fermented wheat beers. However, when used in small quantities it helps round flavours in the beer and assists head formation.
Colour 3–4 EBC, maximum percentage 70%.

Roasted rye malt

An essential for anyone wanting to make a Bavarian-style *roggenbier*. It adds complexity and flavour to many top-fermented beer styles. Use carefully, as it could easily overwhelm some brews.
Colour 800 EBC, maximum percentage 3%.

Spelt

An ancient variety of Bavarian wheat with long, irregularly-shaped kernels. Contains higher protein but lower gluten than wheat malt. Provides a slightly sweet, nutty, spicy flavour. Use like wheat malt.
Colour 3–4 EBC, maximum percentage 70%.

Unmalted grains (adjuncts)

Most unmalted grains are best used in flaked form.

Flaked rice

Virtually flavourless but provides some body without darkening the colour. A highly recommended adjunct, as its low nitrogen content assists in clearing.
Maximum percentage 10%.

Flaked barley

Flaked barley imparts a lovely grainy flavour and can be used in quite large quantities in stouts and porters. However, it can

Cath Harries

cause haze problems in paler styles, where the percentage should not exceed 5%.
Maximum percentage 20%.

Flaked maize

Derived from corn kernels, this cereal gives a delicate corn taste to beer if used sparingly. Its use is beneficial for clearing purposes due to its low nitrogen content.
Maximum percentage 10%.

Flaked oats

An easy-to-use alternative to malted oats. Use for oatmeal stout and sparingly in Belgian *witbier*.
Maximum percentage 10%.

Torrified wheat

Available whole and flaked, this grain is used in small quantities extensively to promote head retention in ales and bitters. Its use is recommended in all recipes where a good firm head is required. Ideal for brewing Belgian *witbier*.
Maximum percentage 10% (or up to 40% for witbier).

Roasted barley

Unmalted barley which has been roasted to a dark colour. It's one of the darkest grains of all. It adds a burnt, bitter taste to beers, as can be found in some stouts. It can also be used in small quantities to darken other beers.
Maximum percentage 10%.

Hops

Most people have no need to use hops, but then they aren't brewers. There's hardly any aspect of beer, its quality and character on which hops don't impact – taste, aroma, colour and microbiological stability are all profoundly influenced.

The managing director of Charles Faram Hops, Paul Corbett, describes hops as the Cinderella of the beer world – though perhaps he would have been better to add they can be the Ugly Sisters too. Even the best brewers are often unsure of the contribution hops will actually make to a beer – it all depends on when they're added and the temperature of the wort or beer.

Hops are used for three separate purposes, besides their natural preserving properties. Firstly, they impart bitterness; secondly, they combine with the malt to give the beer its flavour – and in some beers hops are the main source of flavour; and thirdly, they provide the wonderful aromas associated with the world's best beers. Today the search is on to find more flavoursome hops, and varieties are valued for their citrus, vanilla and other exotic flavours.

Cath Harries

To obtain the maximum bitterness from hops, they need to be boiled in the wort for at least one hour. The alpha acids, which provide the bitterness, are insoluble until they've been isomerised by the long boil. However, all of the aroma in these hops will be lost with the steam. It's for this reason that hops are added at different stages during the boil – typically at the beginning and end.

At the beginning of the boil the bittering/copper hops are added. Although much of their flavour disappears during boiling, each hop variety has its own characteristic bitterness. In general, high alpha hops give a somewhat harsh bitterness, which could be unpleasant in a heavily hopped beer; so high alpha hops should be used instead in mildly hopped beers, or in stouts where the principal flavour is derived from the roasted malt and dark grain.

When creating a beer with a high but often subtle fragrant hop profile, such as traditional English bitters or Pilsners, only the best aroma hops should be used. The aroma hops should be added a few minutes (about five to ten) from the end of the boiling process. To create even more swirls of fragrant aromas, hops can be added into the wort once the boiling is over and left to steep. In some cases the beer is dry-hopped after fermentation, when the hops are added to the conditioning tank or inserted into a keg or cask.

HOP VARIETIES

Generally, hops fall into three broad categories – aroma, dual-purpose and bittering/copper.

Aroma hops are usually low in alpha acids but high in essential oils. Examples include Goldings, Fuggles and Tettanger. The bitterness derived from aroma hops is different from the high alpha varieties such as Target or Northern Brewer.

Dual-purpose hops are high in alpha acids but have some good aromatic qualities. They can be added early or late in the boil, but aren't likely to be suitable for dry hopping.

Bittering/copper hops are used if low bitterness levels are required. They're ideal for use in dark beers made with roasted grains.

Some popular hop varieties (there are many more) include:

AROMA HOPS

Ahtanum

Growing in popularity in the US as an alternative to the pungent Cascade in pale ales and bitters, Ahtanum provides a delightful flowery aroma.
Alpha acid 5–6.5%.

Bramling Cross

Originally bred from the Bramling Golding and a wild American hop, Bramling Cross is a low-yielding variety grown in Kent

Bitterness

When creating a beer its bitterness is important. The bittering strength of the hops is measured by the alpha acid content, represented in a percentage. The higher the percentage, the stronger the hops.

The internationally recognised standard for measuring bitterness in beer is the European Bittering Unit (EBU) or International Bitterness Units (IBU). Most beers fall between IBU 25 and IBU 65.

Some examples of IBU
- Mild, brown ale, wheat beer, British and Munich style lagers – IBU 15–25.
- Pilsner – IBU 28–40.
- Bitter, pale ale, porter – IBU 30–50.
- Irish stout, Imperial stout, barley wine – IBU 40–75.

In the US, many home and commercial craft brewers have set themselves the task of making their beer with the highest possible bitterness. Peter Fowler of the Pitstop Brewery at the Shoulder of Mutton pub in Wantage, Oxfordshire, says his Hop beer at 8% and IBU 323 is the bitterest in the world.

There's a simple formula for determining the weight of hops in grams required to brew to a specified IBU value, and my thanks go to Brupak for giving it to me. The formula assumes a 20% hop utilisation:

$$\frac{\text{IBU required} \times \text{brew length in litres}}{\text{Alpha acid of chosen hops} \times 2}$$

So, if you decide to brew 25 litres of an English-style bitter at EBU 45 using East Kent Goldings, with an alpha acid content of 7.6%, the calculation is as follows:

$$(45 \times 25) \div (7.6 \times 2) = 74\text{gm}$$

When doing the calculation, only the bittering/copper hops should be used, as little or no bitterness will be extracted from late addition hops. If you don't want to do the maths there are plenty of online tools which will do the work for you.

Noble hops

The hops found in many of Europe's classic beers such as Pilsner, *dunkels* and *märzens* are often described as 'noble'. They're low in bitterness and have soft, fragrant and aromatic qualities. Noble hop varieties include Saaz, Hallertauer, Hallertauer Mittelfrüh, Tettnang, Styrian Goldings, Spalt, Perle and Hersbrucker. They have spicy herbal and flowery aromatics and often reveal swathes of citrus zest.

and Sussex. It has a highly distinctive aroma, and even apple characteristics. It works well in darker, stronger beers and is popular with many of the UK's new wave of commercial brewers.
Alpha acid 5–7%.

Cascade

An American hop variety that helped start a taste revolution. Due to its very high levels of essential oils, Cascade has an aroma which is all its own. It's very popular among not just the new breed of American microbrewers, but many brewers in the UK too. The Cascade nose is immediately evident in their beers.
Alpha acid 5–7%.

Centennial

Known as Super Cascade, some of the best American pale ales and IPAs use it for its characteristic powerful hop flavour and aroma.
Alpha acid 6–11%.

Crystal

Bred from Hallertauer Hersbrucker and Cascade, this is a hop of the very highest quality. It's in many beers where a distinct, floral aroma is required.
Alpha acid 4–6%.

East Kent Goldings

Ideal for pale ales and bitter.
Alpha acid 4.5–6%.

First Gold

Another of the new varieties of easier to harvest dwarf hedgerow hops. Its aroma is similar to the Golding. It has a spicy aroma that makes it particularly suitable for late and dry hopping.
Alpha acid 8–9%.

Endeavour

A new hop for brewers to try. It's full of blackcurrant and grapefruit flavours.
Alpha acid 5–9%.

Fuggles

A mainstay of many British bitters but one that also works well in darker ales.
Alpha acid 5–6.5%.

Hallertauer Aroma

Grown in New Zealand, this has a rich aroma that keeps its freshness even in older beers. Perfect for strong lagers and robust bitters.
Alpha acid 7–9.5%.

Hallertauer Hersbrucker

Grown in the Hersbruck district of the Hallertau area in Germany, the largest hop-growing region in the world, this is the classic lager hop. It has a fine, aromatic aroma, and some brewers are using it in golden ales.
Alpha acid 2–5%.

Hallertauer Mittelfrüh

Hallertauer Mittelfrüh is regarded as one of the world's finest aromatic hops. It's a favourite with US brewers and those who make Pilsners.
Alpha acid 3–5.5%.

Liberty

Liberty is bred from Hallertauer Mittelfrüh and retains some of that variety's characteristics. It's being used to great effect in English-style ales, where it displays some Fuggles characteristics.
Alpha acid 3.5–5.5%.

Motueka

A crossbreed of New Zealand varieties and Saaz parentage, this is suited to big Czech-style Pilsners. It has a delightful flavour and a distinctive aroma that can also be used in other styles, particularly Belgian-style ales.
Alpha acid 6.5–7.5%.

Mount Hood

An American variety developed from the German Hallertauer Mittelfrüh hop. It can be readily used in both lagers and ales where a mild aroma is required.
Alpha acid 4–7%.

Perle

Although generally regarded as an aroma hop, the moderately high alpha acid content of this variety finds many brewers using it as a bittering hop in the copper.
Alpha acid 5.5–8.5%.

Progress

Originally grown in England as a Fuggles replacement, Progress is a very versatile hop that combines fine aroma

properties with a respectable alpha acid content. Many brewers say it should be used in conjunction with Goldings in bitters.
Alpha acid 5–7.5%.

Saaz

The classic Pilsner hop from the Czech Republic is used in one of the world's finest beers, Pilsner Urquell. It has a beautiful floral aroma and delicate bitterness, which makes it suitable for many styles. In Germany, the *altbier* brewers of Düsseldorf use handfuls of Saaz to achieve high bitterness levels.
Alpha acid 2–5%.

Sladek

A hop popular with Czech home brewers, it has some notable floral, earthy and spicy notes.
Alpha acid 6–8%.

Sovereign

A low-growing hop and an example of the new hedgerow variety with excellent brewing quality. They can be used with or as a substitute for Fuggles, Goldings or Challenger.
Alpha acid 5–6.5%.

Spalt Select

A classic German-style aromatic hop, which is bred from the famous Hallertauer Mittelfrüh variety. It's used in Pilsner-style beers that need a distinctive but refined hop character.
Alpha acid 3.5–5.5%.

Strisselspalt

A French hop that's gaining favour in the UK. It has some soft floral and herbal notes.
Alpha acid 2–5%.

Styrian Goldings

An English Fuggles hop that was imported to Yugoslavia in the 1930s, when it got its name. It has a perfumed aroma and is ideal for less malty English ales. Many commercial English brewers use these for late and dry hopping bitters.
Alpha acid 3–6%.

Tettnang

A noble hop that's ideal for bitter beers, particularly well-hopped Pilsners from the north of Germany. It's a favourite with brewers wanting high levels of bitterness in their ales.
Alpha acid 2–5%.

Wai-Iti

A New Zealand hop, which is fast gaining popularity with home brewers. It's full of mandarin, lemon and lime zest flavours.
Alpha acid 2–4%.

Whitbread Golding Variety

Originally bred by Whitbread brewery, this variety displays both Goldings and Fuggles characteristics. Although very fine ales can be made using it exclusively, it's more usually used in combination with other varieties.
Alpha acid 5–8%.

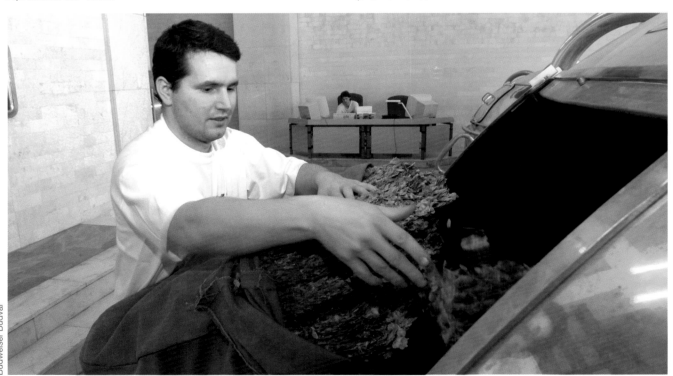

Budweiser Budvar

Willamette

Originally bred from the Fuggle, Willamette it is now an aroma variety in its own right. It has a blackcurrant and herbal aroma that's quite distinctive, and is being used to great effect in many ales.
Alpha acid 4–6%.

Worcester Goldings

The beautiful, flowery Goldings aroma is highly prized by brewers, but supplies are becoming harder to obtain due to poor yields and low resistance to disease.
Alpha acid 5–6.5%.

DUAL-PURPOSE HOPS

Amarillo

An exceptional quality American hop with an orange-citrus flavour. Use sparingly for flavouring, as the orange flavour can dominate. Superb for late or dry hopping.
Alpha acid 8–10%.

Aurora – Slovenia

This hop has an intense but pleasant aroma and is great for bittering. It can be used in all ales and in small amounts in lagers.
Alpha acid 8–10%.

Brewers Gold

Very popular in Germany as a copper hop. Its bitterness is highly suited to lager beers. It's at its best when used in conjunction with noble varieties such as Tettnang and Hallertauer Mittelfrüh.
Alpha acid 5–9%.

Budweiser Budvar

Challenger

Originally developed as a replacement for Goldings, this has fine bittering properties and a respectable aroma when used on its own, but is often combined with a dedicated aroma variety. It's gradually being replaced by the dwarf hop Pioneer.
Alpha acid 5–9%.

Citra

An American hop renowned for its mango, tropical fruit and lime flavours.
Alpha acid 11–14%.

Dr Rudi

A New Zealand hop which is full of lemon grass, pine needle and some grassy flavours.
Alpha acid 11–14%.

Green Bullet

Exceptional quality New Zealand hop which has a pleasant aroma as well as a very high alpha acid content. It can be substituted for Styrian Goldings.
Alpha acid 11–13%.

Nelson Sauvin

A New Zealand hop that's growing in popularity with craft brewers. It has sweeping gooseberry and grapefruit notes.
Alpha acid 10–13%.

Northdown

A seedling of Northern Brewer, which is no longer grown in Britain. Although Northdown can be used on its own, especially in darker styles of beer such as stouts, it's the ideal accompaniment to aroma hops such as Fuggles or Progress.
Alpha acid 7–10%.

Pilgrim

A newish hop, Pilgrim is proving popular as an alternative to more traditional high-alpha hops such as Northdown and Northern Brewer. It's a true dual-purpose hop, as besides its high bittering power it possesses excellent aromatic properties.
Alpha acid 11–12.5%.

Pioneer

Pioneer is one of the new breed of dwarf hops. It has a fine aroma and a delicate bitterness.
Alpha acid 8.5–9.5%.

Simcoe

A very versatile hop, as it possesses high bittering power with a somewhat unique, pine-like aroma. It can be detected in many classic American ales.
Alpha acid 12–14%.

Tim Hampson

Sorachi Ace

An American hop that's being increasingly used in Europe, even by the highly traditional Duvel brewery in Belgium. It's full of lemon and coconut flavours.
Alpha acid 10–14%.

Pacific Gem

Although it has one of the highest alpha acid contents in the world, this New Zealand hop has a delicious berry-fruit aroma much prized by many brewers. More suited to ales than lagers.
Alpha acid 14–18%.

Stella

An Australian hop that's been used by the renowned English craft brewer Thornbridge. It's full of cedar, peach and apricot flavours.
Alpha acid 14–16%.

Wakatu

One of the new wave of New Zealand hops, it has vanilla, floral and lime notes.
Alpha acid 7–10%.

BITTERING HOPS

Admiral

Very high alpha acid content and a mild flavour make Admiral the bittering hop of choice for many brewers. Best in conjunction with more flavourful finishing hops.
Alpha acid 13–16%.

Magnum – Germany

A very clean bittering hop with little flavour and aroma. Very popular with lager brewers for base bitterness, but also finding favour with brewers of ales. Excellent when used with noble hops.
Alpha acid 12–14%.

Northern Brewer – Germany

Although originally developed in Britain, Northern Brewer is now grown almost exclusively in Germany. It can be used to provide bitterness in both ales and lagers. Its low aroma requires it to be used with other, more flavourful hops for the best results.
Alpha acid 10–11%.

Target

Target is by far the most widely grown variety in Britain. Although seen by many brewers as an aroma hop, it's at its best in the copper producing beers with a low bitterness. Used with discretion in combination with fine aroma hops, however, excellent bitters and pale ales can be produced.
Alpha acid 10–11.5%.

Cath Harries

Home brewing kits: some troubleshooting

Symptom	Possible causes	Reason and solutions
Fermentation has failed to start		
• No bubbles or froth on the surface of the wort. • No characteristic fermentation odour. • No activity through the airlock.	• Wort too cold (yeast dormant). • Wort too hot (yeast stunned/ killed). • Old yeast (expired – check 'best before' date). • The lid and/or the airlock of the fermenter aren't sealing adequately or aren't screwed down tight enough. • Forgot to add the yeast.	• Pitching the yeast into wort that's too cold or has been allowed to become too cold may prevent or significantly slow down fermentation. Move the fermenter to a warmer place (18–23°C) and rouse the yeast by stirring the wort with a sterilised spoon. • Pitching yeast into wort that's too hot (>35°C) or has been allowed to become too hot may kill or stun the yeast, resulting in slow or no fermentation. Move the fermenter to a cooler place. When the wort has cooled to 18–24°C, stir in another sachet of yeast. • Dried yeast has a finite life and can lose its viability over time, especially if exposed to the air or moisture. Always ensure the sachet of yeast is within its 'best before' date and not damaged. Always store yeast sachets in a cool, dry place. Stir in a new sachet of yeast. • If the airlock and/or fermenter lid isn't sealed then there'll be no active bubbling through the airlock. The wort may actually be fermenting, but the CO_2 gas will be escaping through the faulty seal. Fermentation can be verified by removing the fermenter lid and examining the wort. Indicators of fermentation are: condensation inside the lid, frothing/bubbling of the surface of the wort, and a ring of scum on the fermenter wall above the wort. Rectify the faulty seal. Ensure fermenter lid is pushed down tightly. • Are you sure you added the yeast?
Frothing through the airlock		
• Froth rising out of the fermenter airlock.	• A vigorous fermentation. • Overfilling of fermenter.	• There's no need for concern – apart from a bit of a mess, it's actually a good sign, and indicates that the yeast is strong and fermenting vigorously. • If overfilling is the cause, drain off some of the wort using a sterilised siphon. • Clean and refill the airlock with water and allow the yeast to continue fermenting the brew. Frothing over can be avoided by using a larger fermenter.

Symptom	Possible causes	Reason and solutions
Stuck fermentation		
• The beer hasn't reached the expected final gravity (the gravity reading hasn't changed over a period of three–four days but is still too high for bottling or barrelling). • This might be accompanied by no visible signs of continuing fermentation and no bubbles rising through the airlock.	• Poor ingredients (poorly fermentable wort). • Insufficient yeast nutrients. • Old yeast. • Temperature shock. • Fluctuating temperature. • High alcohol levels. • Wrong strain of yeast.	• Poor ingredients may result in a high proportion of complex carbohydrates relative to the proportion of simple carbohydrates (sugars) in the wort. It's much easier for yeast to ferment simple sugars. High levels of complex carbohydrates will cause the fermentation to slow down considerably once the simple sugars have been used up. It may be possible for the yeast to ferment these but it can take a long time (several weeks). Hence the fermentation may appear to become stuck. • Insufficient nitrogen nutrients can cause yeast to stop working. This can occur with poor ingredients and with beers that are made using very high percentages of refined sugars, such as ordinary household sugar. These sugars won't contain sufficient nutrients and will have a diluting effect on the nutrients provided by the other ingredients. For kits that require additional sugar, don't use more than is stated in the kit instructions. Stirring a yeast nutrient (available from home brew suppliers) into the brew may help to rectify the problem. Alternatively, use an all malt extract kit. • Temperature shock can cause yeast to stop working. If the temperature is allowed to become too hot during the fermentation, it can kill the yeast. If it's allowed to become too cold it will result in very slow fermentation or no fermentation at all. • The ideal fermentation temperature is 18–23°C. • Yeast doesn't like rapid fluctuations in temperature. Even fluctuations within this range can cause yeast to slow down or stop working. The temperature should be kept as constant as possible throughout the fermentation period. • High alcohol levels inhibit and eventually kill yeast. Alcohol is a by-product of fermentation and the level gradually increases in the wort during fermentation. Different yeast strains can survive different levels of alcohol. • If the brew is a high gravity brew, then conventional ale yeasts will be inhibited by the increasing alcohol level before all of the sugars have been fermented. This will result in a high final gravity reading and a very sweet-tasting beer. It's important that an appropriate strain of high alcohol tolerant yeast is used for such brews. Whilst it may be tempting to ignore kit instructions and add extra sugar in an attempt to increase alcohol levels, it's unwise, because this may result in a high final gravity and also compromise the quality of the final beer. It's important that kit instructions are followed as intended. • It might not always be possible to restart a stuck fermentation, but the following actions are often successful: • Ensure the temperature of the brew is 18–23°C. Gently stir the brew to rouse the yeast, using a sterilised stirrer/spoon. This action alone will often start the yeast working again. • Add a new sachet of yeast to the brew. This should first be rehydrated and activated by mixing the dried yeast into a glass of pre-boiled, lukewarm water together with a teaspoon of sugar. This should be covered and left in a warm place until seen to be actively fermenting, before stirring it into the main brew. • Use a good-quality brewing yeast designed for all-malt recipe brews that's capable of fermenting out higher or complex sugars.
High final gravity		
• Hydrometer reading is high after the fermentation has finished.	• Stuck fermentation. • High original gravity (a high gravity brew). • Inaccurate hydrometer. • Incorrect use of hydrometer.	• A stuck fermentation will result in a high gravity reading (see *Stuck fermentation*). • High gravity brews will usually have a higher final gravity than lower gravity brews. A high gravity brew may be intentional (which will be indicated on the kit instructions), or may be a result of adding extra sugar to the brew (either accidentally or deliberately). • Is the hydrometer accurate? This can be checked using water – the reading should be 1.000 at 20°C. • Be sure to read the hydrometer correctly (at the bottom of the meniscus) and at the correct temperature (20°C) – refer to your hydrometer instructions.

Symptom	Possible causes	Reason and solutions
Beer won't clear		
• Beer looks cloudy, hazy or foggy.	• Insufficient clearing time allowed. • The nature of the yeast strain. • Type of beer. • Excess complex carbohydrates in beer (poor ingredients). • Contamination by wild yeasts or bacteria. • Chill haze (see *Chill haze*).	• When beer is bottled or barrelled it will always display a degree of cloudiness caused by the millions of yeast cells in suspension. This is a good thing, because the yeast is required for fermenting the priming sugar. Normally the brew will clear once the yeast has performed the secondary fermentation (adding fizz to the beer) and has been allowed to stand undisturbed. Clearing usually takes around two weeks, but can vary significantly – so be patient. • A brew that doesn't clear is still likely to be drinkable in many cases. Taste it and see. • Some strains of yeast don't settle as completely as others. The serious brewer might wish to experiment with different strains. • Some types of beer, by their nature, aren't meant to clear or won't clear completely. Most German wheat beers are examples of this. • If the beer contains excessive amounts of complex carbohydrates and proteins it may not clear completely. This is usually a result of poor-quality ingredients, but the beer may still be perfectly drinkable. • A fining agent (available from home brew suppliers) can aid clearing in many cases. Follow the instructions supplied. • If the brew is contaminated by wild yeasts or bacteria it's unlikely to clear. It may also be undrinkable (see *Spoiled/infected beer*).
Poor head retention		
• Poor head – beer has a flat appearance. • Head doesn't last and fades very quickly. • Head doesn't form.	• Dirty glassware. • Under-carbonation. • Residual sterilant or detergent in the bottles or barrel. • High alcohol content. • Too little protein and complex carbohydrates in the wort.	• Dirty glassware is by far the most common cause. Grease, salt, soap residue and detergent will kill the head on the beer. The beer glass may be dirty, or may not have been rinsed thoroughly after washing. Ensure glassware is spotlessly clean. • Also, if the beer is being drunk with greasy or salty food or snacks, the grease or salt will make its way from the food to your lips to the beer, and the head will suffer its effects. • The beer may not be fully carbonated (see *Under-carbonation*). • Residual sterilant or detergent in the bottles/barrel will have the same effect as dirty glassware (see above). Ensure these are thoroughly rinsed with cold tap water prior to filling. • Beer with a high alcohol content is usually the result of adding an excess (more than 1kg) of ordinary sugar to the wort. This has the effect of thinning down the body of the final beer by diluting the proteins and complex carbohydrates that are responsible for head retention (ordinary sugar is too pure and doesn't contain these). If a high alcohol beer is required it's best to use a malt extract powder instead of ordinary sugar. Malt extract will give more body and aid head retention.

Tim Hampson

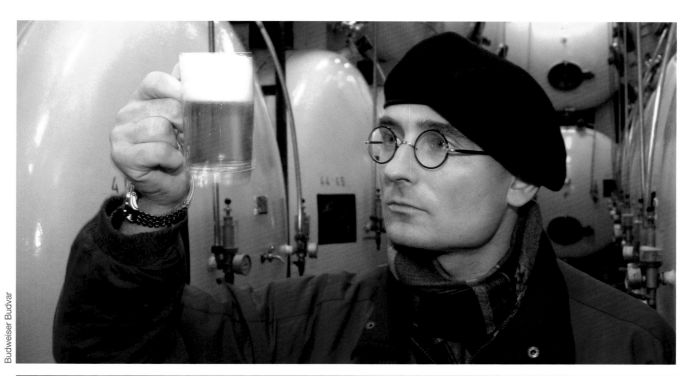

Budweiser Budvar

Symptom	Possible causes	Reason and solutions
Spoiled/infected beer		
• Unusual taste and smell (vinegar, sour, wet cardboard, mouldy, musty, TCP). • Beer cloudy – although this isn't always a sign of infection (see *Beer won't clear*). • A ring of scum on the inside neck of beer bottles, near the beer line. • Mould on surface of brew.	• Contamination by bacteria or wild yeasts from inadequately cleaned and sterilised brewing equipment. • Contamination by bacteria, wild yeasts or mould spores from the air.	*Cleanliness is essential...* • It's the home brewer's constant challenge to prevent contamination by spoilage organisms. A comprehensive cleaning and sanitising regime will reduce the number of potential spoilage organisms to a minimum but will never eradicate them completely. • It's essential that all brewing equipment that comes into contact with the beer is thoroughly cleaned and sterilised before use. Various sterilising and cleaning agents are available from home brew suppliers, and the instructions should be carefully followed. • Scouring pads or stiff brushes shouldn't be used to clean brewing equipment, particularly the fermenter. This is because such items will leave minute scratches on the walls that create an ideal place for bacteria to harbour, thereby increasing the chances of the brew becoming infected. The inside of the fermenter should only be cleaned with a soft cloth, and any caked-on residues soaked off rather than scrubbed. • Once the brew has been mixed (concentrate/sugar/water) there shouldn't be any delay in adding the yeast. The faster the yeast starts to work, the less chance of contamination (because the yeast will compete against potential spoilage organisms). Often brewers use too much hot water and then wait for the wort temperature to fall before pitching the yeast. This is a critical time for potential spoilage organisms to gain a foothold – the longer the delay, the more likely the brew will become infected. It's far better to get the temperature correct to start with, which should be around 18–23°C. Follow the beer kit instructions carefully. • Avoid exposing the brew to the air. Ensure the lid is put on to the fermenter as soon as the ingredients have been dissolved and the yeast has been added. It should only be necessary to remove the lid and expose the brew when taking hydrometer readings and during bottling or barrelling. Keep windows closed when brewing. Don't leave the beer in the fermenter for overly extended periods. • Despite a high standard of hygiene it's still possible to experience a bad brew. This is because there will always be airborne bacteria and wild yeasts present when preparing, fermenting and bottling/barrelling a brew. It's just bad luck. • It isn't possible to save a bad brew, so discard it. Clean and sterilise the brewing equipment thoroughly and start again.

Cath Harries

Symptom	Possible causes	Reason and solutions
Over-carbonation		
• Very gassy and foaming beer. • Beer gushing when bottles are opened. • Very frothy or too much head. • Exploding beer bottles.	• Too much priming sugar. • Beer bottled or barrelled too early. • Poor sterilisation of bottles or barrel. • Overfilling of bottles.	• Over-carbonation is usually associated with bottled beer. It's a lesser problem with barrelled beer because barrels usually have a pressure relief valve. • The use of too much priming sugar will result in over-carbonation. Measure and dispense the priming sugar carefully. For bottles use half a level teaspoon in each bottle. For barrels use 80g. • It's important not to bottle or barrel the beer too early before the initial fermentation has finished. In this situation unfermented sugars are carried over into the bottle, and when combined with the priming sugar (already in the bottle) excess gas is produced. If the gas pressure is high enough glass bottles will explode. Always check the brew with a hydrometer to ensure fermentation is complete prior to bottling. • Poor sterilisation of the bottles or barrel may allow the beer to come into contact with wild yeast, which can result in over-carbonation and possibly off flavours. Ensure the bottles or barrel are thoroughly sterilised. Then thoroughly rinse with cold tap water before filling with beer. • Bottles should be filled to allow 15mm of head space.
Under-carbonation		
• Flat beer. • Poor head.	• Forgotten to add priming sugar. • Not enough priming sugar added. • Faulty bottle or barrel seals. Bottle caps not tight enough. Barrel lid not screwed down tight enough. • Sterilising solution remaining in bottles or barrel. • Bottles or barrel being stored at low temperature during secondary fermentation stage.	• Remember to add the priming sugar. Use the correct amount in the barrel or each bottle to ensure sufficient secondary fermentation. For bottles use half a level teaspoon in each bottle. For barrels use 80g. • Ensure bottle caps and barrel seals aren't faulty (ie they're clean, undamaged and fully seated). Ensure bottle caps are crimped down tightly. Ensure barrel lid is screwed down tightly. • Traces of sterilising solution can kill the yeast, resulting in no secondary fermentation. Ensure the barrel or bottles are thoroughly rinsed with cold tap water after sterilisation. • Store the bottles or barrel in a warm place (18–23°C) for seven days to ensure secondary fermentation. After this time they may be moved to a cooler place to settle and clear.

Symptom	Possible causes	Reason and solutions
Chill haze		
• Bottled beer develops a haze or cloudiness if chilled or stored in the fridge.	• Cold temperatures (< 7°C) resulting in the interaction of proteins and polyphenols in the beer.	• Most beers will be clear at room temperature but some will develop a haze when refrigerated. This is due to haze-producing proteins and polyphenols (primarily from the malt) suspended in the beer. When the beer is chilled these react and clump into tiny particles, which reflect light. These particles remain in suspension and make the beer appear hazy. • Chill haze doesn't affect the taste of beer – only the appearance. • It's a common problem with home brewers and some beer kits. • Allowing the bottles to warm back to room temperature may reduce the haze. Alternatively, leaving the bottles upright and undisturbed in the refrigerator for a few weeks will allow time for the protein to settle to the bottom of the bottles, and the beer may eventually clear. Other than that, there isn't anything practical that can be done to avoid it. Commercial breweries and serious home brewers who produce fully-mashed beers can eliminate this problem using various techniques. For home brewers who use beer kits the technicalities would become impractical for the hobby. • Just enjoy the beer for what it is, or drink it out of a pewter or ceramic stein if the appearance bothers you.
Sediment		
• A narrow layer of sediment at the bottom of the bottles.	• Yeast sediment.	• This is perfectly normal for bottle-conditioned beer, which relies on the yeast to ferment the priming sugar and produce gas. The sediment is the result of the yeast settling out of suspension after the secondary fermentation has finished. • The layer of sediment is typically 3mm. A thicker layer of sediment may indicate that the beer was bottled too early (*ie* before the primary fermentation was finished). It may also be the result of accidentally siphoning over some of the sediment from the bottom of the fermenter. Care should be taken to avoid siphoning any of the sediment from the fermenter during the bottling/barrelling stage. Leaving beer on a thick layer of sediment can result in off flavours developing during storage (see *Unusual taste*).

Beer Genie

Symptom	Possible causes	Reason and solutions
Unusual taste		
• The beer has an unusual taste and/or smell. • A wide range of unusual flavours can occur in beer – vinegary, cheesy, sweaty, rancid, earthy, musty, rusty, skunky, rotten eggs, rotten vegetables, sour, medicinal, etc.	• Spoilage/ infected beer. • Exposure to light. • High fermentation temperature. • Fluctuations in fermentation temperature. • Yeast and yeast breakdown. • Old/overaged beer.	• A very wide range of unusual (and unpleasant) flavours can be caused by spoilage from bacteria, moulds and wild yeasts (see *Spoiled/infected beer*). • Exposure of beer to light can cause a skunky flavour. Light has a very adverse effect on the bittering components of hops, which can produce this off flavour. If the beer is bottled it should always be in brown bottles, never those which are clear or green. It's most common amongst light-coloured beers which are heavily hopped (because light penetrates the beer more easily). Direct sunlight and fluorescent tubes are the worst offenders. Store the beer in a cool dark place to prevent this. • High fermentation temperatures and fluctuations in temperature can cause off flavours to be produced (fruity, solvent). Ensure fermentation is carried out at the correct temperature (18–23°C) and avoid fluctuations. • When pouring home-bottled beer into a glass, do this slowly and avoid disturbing the natural yeast sediment (which can give a yeasty or tangy flavour). It's best to leave 1cm or so of beer in the bottle to prevent this from being poured into the glass. • Yeast breakdown can result in off flavours (*eg* rotten vegetables, meaty, marmite). This is a common result of leaving the beer in the fermenter for too long, sitting on that layer of dead yeast. Barrelled beer, if kept for too long, can also be affected in this way. Don't keep the beer in the fermenter after the fermentation has finished. Similarly, don't keep barrelled beer for a long period. • The flavour of beer will also naturally change with age. This may be beneficial for some high gravity beers and barley wine, which may improve with age, but for ordinary beers it's best to drink them within a reasonable time (not usually a problem for home brewers). • In general, bottled beer will keep for longer periods than cask beer.

[With thanks to Muntons.]

Keeping a brewing log

The better the records you keep, the better the brewer you become, so it's important to keep records on the ingredients and quantities used, temperatures, times, and even your perceptions of the beer. There are several brewing spreadsheets and software programs available on the Internet that can be a big help, but doing it yourself using something like Excel software is fine too.

Keeping a brewing log is important, as it gives you the opportunity to recreate good brews and to avoid repeating those with which you were dissatisfied. A good start is to write up each recipe in a consistent manner, such as this recipe, created by Paul Carrruthers, which won a home brewing competition organised by the Thornbridge Brewery.

Paul believes his success was down to scrupulous attention to detail in all areas, particularly sanitation. He advises other home brewers to be open-minded and sample as many different styles as they can, and then brew them. 'Don't be afraid to experiment,' says Paul, 'this is the advantage home brewers have over commercial brewers – we can try anything without too much risk.'

BEER: FRANK AS APOLLO

Fermentable	Colour	Grams	Ratio
Pale malt	5 EBC	4,230g	85%
Munich malt	20 EBC	495g	10%
Caramunich II	124 EBC	245g	5%

Hop variety	Type	Alpha	Time	grams	Ratio
Simcoe	Whole	12.7%	90min	13g	10.8%
Simcoe	Whole	12.7%	15min	20g	16.2%
Apollo	Whole	19.5%	15min	20g	16.2%
Apollo	Whole	19.5%	0min	46g	37.8%
Columbus (Tomahawk)	Whole	15%	0min	23g	18.9%

Final volume	25 litres
Original gravity	1.046
Final gravity	1.011
Alcohol content	4.5% ABV
Total liquor	35.5 litres
Mash liquor	12.5 litres
Mash efficiency	77%
Bitterness	47 EBU
Colour	19 EBC

Yeast – WLP001, US–05 or equivalent
Mash at 68°C for 60 minutes. Boil for 90 minutes.
Ferment at 20°C.

BREWER'S LOG

Information could include:

- Beer style/name.
- Start time.
- End of primary fermentation.
- End of secondary fermentation.
- Cask/kegging date.
- Bottling date.
- Recipe.
- Batch size.
- Anticipated OG.
- Grist composition.
- Hop schedule.
- Yeast.
- Temperature of wort at time of pitch.
- Mash procedure.
- Mash duration.
- Water/mash ratio.
- Mash volume.
- Estimated absorption.
- Target mash temperature.
- Strike water temperature.
- Mash temperature actual.

Mash/ sparge step	Infusion volume	Infusion temp.	Mash temp.	Volume of runnings	Gravity of runnings
First					
Second					
Third					
Total water					

- Preboil gravity.
- Mash efficiency.

- Boil duration time.
- Irish moss (finings) added.
- Volume pre-boil.
- Volume post-boil.

- Fermentation.
- Fermentation temperature check 1.
- Fermentation temperature check 2.
- Fermentation temperature check 3.
- Final gravity (FG).

- Packaging – cask, keg or bottle.
- Carbonation added.

- Comments on brew.

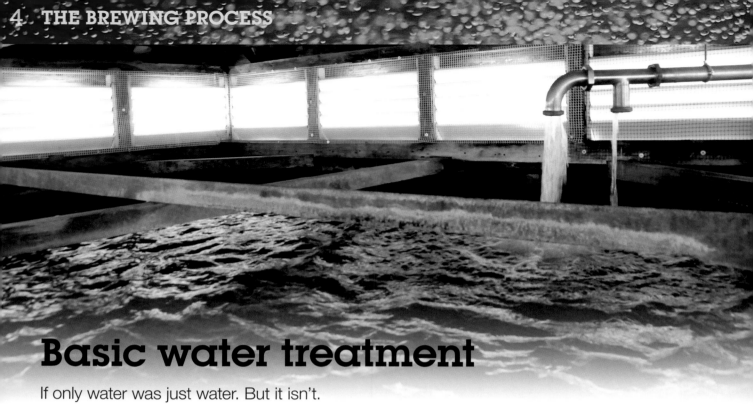

Basic water treatment

If only water was just water. But it isn't.

It's possible to make a beer using water straight from the tap. However, a little tinkering with the water can dramatically improve the quality of your brews. Don't be daunted – water treatment is easy, though you can also make it one of the most complicated elements of brewing good beer. For beginners the best advice is, as always, keep it simple.

Most brewers brew with tap water, though a commercial brewer might call it the 'town supply' or 'town water'. However, whatever your source (some brewers have their own spring or well), a little understanding of what's in the water helps.

Tap water contains chlorine, which kills off bugs. It's important, even for people using a basic home brew kit, to remove this, as it could kill the yeast or taint the beer. The removal of chlorine is easy. Leaving your water standing overnight in an open bucket or other vessel removes it. However, most tap water also contains another group of chemicals called chloramines, which are also used as disinfectants. The chloramines could be boiled away, but it takes time and isn't an efficient use of energy. So you'll have to either pass your water through a carbon filter or simply add a Campden tablet to it. Adding a Campden tablet per 22 litres of brewing water will remove both chlorine and chloramines almost immediately.

Some home brewers prefer to use a Campden tablet containing potassium metabisulfite rather than sodium metabisulfite, as they say the sodium can add off flavours to beer.

MALT EXTRACT AND WATER

If you're brewing using grains or a malt extract then ideally the water needs a bit more treatment.

You'll need to know if your water is hard or soft. If you get fur/scale at the bottom of your kettle – it looks like a crusty white deposit – then the water is hard. This means it contains calcium bicarbonate (chalk). If it's left at high levels it will increase the acidity of your wort and bring out harsher flavours from hops, and it could even stop the yeast working properly. The scale can also damage your heating elements if they come in contact with it.

To soften your water you can add a carbonate-reducing salt – your home brewer supplier will sell you this. An alternative is to boil the water for about 15 minutes, and when it's cooled you siphon or pour off the water you need for brewing and leave the sediment at the bottom of the boiler.

However, a certain amount of calcium sulphate (gypsum) can be a good thing in water. Burton upon Trent became home to so many breweries because of its plentiful supply of gypsum-rich water, which bubbled up through the aquifer into the town's many wells, and is ideal for the production of pale ales. Consequently many brewers add gypsum to their brewing water if they're brewing ales. The process is often called 'burtonising'. Your home brewer supplier will sell you gypsum – a couple of teaspoons per 22 litres of water is normally enough.

If you want to be more scientific, then find out the level of acidity or alkalinity of your water (this is known as its pH). Most tap water has a pH of around 7.0, but the enzymes that are present in malt – needed to convert the starch to sugar – prefer the pH to be 5.2–5.6. Once you have established the pH, the precise amount of gypsum which you need to add can be calculated using one of the many water treatment calculators available online.

So, how do you design a beer?

It's probably the most creative and rewarding part of home brewing, and involves much more than simply throwing a bunch of stuff into a mash tun.

One of Italy's most creative brewers, Agostino Arioli of Birrificio Italiano, who started off brewing at home when he was 16, says it's important to have an understanding of the brewing process, and to appreciate every detail of it and what it'll do to the ingredients, when you're designing a new beer. It's a maxim that has served him well, as Tipopils, his crisp, beautifully hopped version of a pils, is regarded as one of the best in the world.

And when Mikkeller founders, former home brewers Mikkel Borg Bjergso and Kristian Klarup Keller, created their astonishing stout, Beer Geek Breakfast, it wasn't just a scattergun approach that saw them choose seven different malts and roasted barley and oats. They understood the attributes of each of the ingredients. Coffee was added to the beer too, and they spent hours making coffee to achieve the taste they were looking for. But even extreme beers need some balance, and the almost overbearing weight of dark malts and coffee flavours is kept in check by an astounding bouquet of citrus from Centennial and Cascade hops.

▼ **Professor of Biotechnology, Frederic Sannier, explains the brewing process to students at the Science Infuse brewery, La Rochelle Science University, France.** (Getty Images)

According to Sharp's creative head brewer Stuart Howe, designing a beer isn't easy because of the thousands of flavour compounds which are in a beer. He says there are various stages to designing a beer:

- Concept.
- Definition.
- Specification.
- Recipe.
- Pilot brew.
- Full-scale brew.
- Marketing.

And if one of the big commercial brewers is thinking of a new beer it's likely to follow this process:

- Market research.
- Focus group.
- Attribute specification.
- Pilots.
- Focus groups.
- Full-scale brew.

A microbrewery is likely to follow a different process, and a new beer is first conceived after a few beers in a pub:

- The brew itself is often the first step in the process.
- Concept is developed by the brewer.
- The focus group is just one or two people, probably whoever's in the brewery.
- Pilot brew may be sold.
- Whether it's brewed again depends on sales.
- The brewer's palate and understanding of the market's palate needs to be excellent.
- Product is personal to the brewer.

According to Hall & Woodhouse head brewer Toby Heasman, people developing a new beer shouldn't be scared, they should be brave. A new beer gives the brewer the opportunity to experiment with:

- Malt flavour and colour.
- Hops.
- Yeast.
- Alcohol by volume.

But there's much more to it – other things need to be considered: bitterness, sweetness, balance, plus novel ingredients, and when they can be added into the brewing process. Toby says the home brewer needs to consider if the beer is light, dark, malty or biscuity; hoppy, estery bitter or sweet; strong or weak; and if it has any novel flavours.

So how does a home brewer go about developing a beer? Many start by choosing their favourite style or one that interests them. The list on beer styles in this book is a starting place.

However, more guidance can be found on the American Brewers Association website at www.brewersassociation.org. Here can be found the specifications for more than 140 different beer styles. These include well-known styles like IPA wheat and stout, but they also includes rarities such as Adambier and Grätzer, both historic pre-*Reinheitsgebot* styles; they're smoky ales, with the former thriving in and around Dortmund, Germany, and the latter brewed primarily in Poland.

The guidelines focus first on appearance, aroma, flavour and finish, in that order. They also include vital statistics on each of the styles, including ranges for original gravity, apparent extract/final gravity, alcohol by weight/volume, bitterness and colour.

The next step is to choose the ingredients. It's useful to find out what ingredients go into the beer you want to make. Is it German malt, and if so in what proportions? And what hops are used, and when are they added? Various online websites can help with this.

Once you've decided on your ingredients you need to think about the approximate proportions of each. A starting point for malt might be 80% pale malt, 15% caramel malt and 5%

chocolate malt. To make life easier there are a number of online sites that can help with this too, including www.beersmith.com, www.brewersfriend.com, www.hbd.org/recipator and others. You simply enter your ingredients into their online spreadsheets and see what happens.

Using an online program means you have to consider certain factors:

- Original gravity (OG): This is a measure of how much fermentable and unfermentable material is in the beer (sugar). The original gravity of the wort, prior to fermentation, determines how much potential alcohol you have.
- Bitterness (IBUs): Hop bitterness, measured in international bitterness units, is important, as it balances the flavour of malt in the beer.
- Colour: Different malts add different-coloured hues to the beer. Dark malts make a beer blacker, pales ones make them lighter.
- You'll also need to think about the bitterness ratio of the beer – a hoppy beer will have a high ratio, while a malty beer will have a low one.
- Final gravity (FG) of the beer: This is a bit of a moving target – it all depends on the yeast chosen and how much sugar it eats. A highly attenuated beer, one where the yeast eats most of the sugars, is likely to have a clean flavour, while a low attenuation is likely to lead to more complex flavours.
- You'll also have to give thought to how many bubbles you want in your beer. Typically an English mild has low carbonation whereas a German wheat beer is full of carbon dioxide.
- In the mash tun: The temperature of the mash tun for partial and full mash brewing is crucial. The lower the temperature, the lower the body of the beer. The higher the temperature, the higher the body.
- Hops: When do you add them in? Different beer styles demand different methods. Early in the boil, at the last moment or after fermentation? It all depends on what you're looking for.
- Fermentation and conditioning: The temperature of the fermenting wort should be appropriate for the yeast being used. You'll also need to consider how long the beer you're making needs to be conditioned for, and at what temperature; and if you're wood ageing it, what you're going to put it into.

You should never be afraid to experiment with ingredients – and to take the time to discover the attributes of each.

At the Mikkeller brewery, Mikkel Borg Bjergso developed a simple base malt mash, and then went on to brew a series of single varietal hopped beers, to find out the characteristics of each. It's the attention to detail that makes the good stand out from the crowd.

But ultimately the choice is yours. You can just go for it – but if you do, then remember to keep good records. You just might want to brew it again.

Beer recipes

SOME SIMPLE RECIPES – USING MALT EXTRACT

Best Bitter

22 litres
1.8kg Muntons or other light liquid malt extract
250g crystal malt
1kg brewing sugar
110g Goldings hops
Ale yeast

- Boil liquid malt, crystal malt and hops in approximately 14 litres of water.
- After 30 minutes' boiling, strain off into a sterilised bucket and add the brewing sugar. Stir until the sugar dissolves.
- Make up to 22 litres with cold water and leave to cool below 24°C.
- Add yeast and leave to ferment for about seven days or until the fermentation has stopped and no more bubbles are rising.
- Siphon off into a barrel or bottles using half a teaspoon of sugar per 500ml to prime bottles or 50 to 100g if putting into a pressure barrel.
- Leave in a warm place for five days then move into a cool place to clear.

Blonde Bitter

22 litres
1.5kg Coopers or other light malt extract
1kg brewing sugar
110g Cascade hops
Blonde ale yeast

- Boil malt extract and 75g of hops in 14 litres of water. After 50 minutes' boiling add the remaining hops (35g) and continue boiling for 10 more minutes.
- Strain into a clean container, add the sugar and stir until it dissolves.
- Make up to 22 litres with cold water and leave to cool below 24°C.
- To ferment and finish, complete as for Best Bitter (left).

Haynes Golden Ale

22 litres
1.8kg Muntons or other light liquid malt extract
1kg brewing sugar
110g Saaz hops
Lager yeast

- Boil malt and hops for 30 minutes in 14 litres of water.
- Sieve or strain the liquid and add the sugar and dissolve.
- Make up to 22 litres by adding cold water and leave to cool below 24°C.
- To ferment and finish, complete as for Best Bitter (left).

Dark Mild

22 litres
1.8kg Muntons or other dark liquid malt extract
250g crystal malt
1kg brewing sugar
55g Fuggles hops
Ale yeast

- Boil liquid malt, crystal malt and hops in 14 litres of water for 30 minutes.
- Strain or sieve, add the sugar and dissolve.
- Make up to 22 litres and leave to cool below 24°C.
- To ferment and finish, complete as for Best Bitter (P135).

India Pale Ale

22 litres
2 x Coopers 1.5kg light malt extract
500g Muntons light dried malt
50g crushed crystal malt
500g brewing sugar
100g Cascade hops
25g Goldings hops
Ale yeast

- Mix the liquid malt, dried malt and sugar with at least 14 litres of hot water and stir well to dissolve. Bring up to the boil.
- Add the Cascade hops and the crystal malt and boil for 40 minutes. Add extra water if a lot is boiled off.
- Add the Goldings and boil for 10 minutes.
- Leave to cool and then strain into the fermenting vessel.
- Make up to 22 litres with cold water. When the temperature is below 24°C add the yeast.
- To ferment and finish, complete as for Best Bitter (above), but leave to condition for four weeks. The addition of finings will help clarity.
  (With thanks to www.thebrewshop.com.)

CAMRA

Hobsons Brewery

FULL MASH BEER RECIPES

Bitter 3.5% alcohol by volume

25 litres
Original gravity 1.035
Final gravity 1.006

Malt bill
Maris Otter Pale Ale malt 3.6kg
Crystal malt 0.5kg

Hops
Target 11%aa 27g
Golding 5.5%aa 20g
Styrian Golding 4.8%aa 30g

- Infusion mash at 65°C and stand for 60 minutes, 2.5:1 liquor to grist ratio (10.25 litres).
- Sparge with 20 litres of liquor at 80°C.
- Boil for 60 minutes with Target as bittering hops, and add both Goldings 15–10 minutes before boil end.
- Whirlpool and ferment with a good British ale yeast for 3–5 days before cooling.
  (© Mattias Sjoberg Compass Brewery)

Stout 5% ABV

25 litres
Original gravity 1.048
Final gravity 1.010

Malt bill
Pale Ale 4.5kg
Crystal 0.6kg
Flaked barley 0.3kg
Roasted barley 0.3kg

Hops
First Gold 7.3%aa 60g

■ Infusion mash at 65°C and stand for 60 minutes, 2.5:1 liquor to grist ratio (10.25 litres).
■ Sparge with 20 litres of liquor at 80°C.
■ Boil for 60 minutes with First Gold from the start.
■ Whirlpool and ferment with an Irish or London ale yeast for 3–5 days before cooling.

(© Mattias Sjoberg Compass Brewery)

British IPA 6.0%

25 litres
Original gravity 1.055
Final gravity 1.009

Malt bill
Pale ale 6.5kg
Caramalt 0.86kg
Wheat malt 0.38kg

Hops
Bramling Cross 6%aa 100g
Progress 6.5%aa 40g
Golding 4.5%aa 40g

Dry hop
Brewers Gold 5.4%aa 50g

■ Infusion mash at 65°C and stand for 60 minutes, 2.5:1 liquor to grist ratio (10.25 litres).
■ Sparge with 20 litres of liquor at 80°C.
■ Boil for 60 minutes with Bramling Cross as bittering hops, and add Goldings and Progress 15–10 minutes before boil end.
■ Whirlpool and ferment with a good British ale yeast for 5–7 days before cooling.
■ Once primary fermentation is done add the Brewers Gold and store for 7–10 days before filling in bottles or kegs.

(© Mattias Sjoberg Compass Brewery)

Belgian-style Witbier

25 litres
Original gravity 1.060
Final gravity 1.018
ABV 5.5%
Mash liquor – 14.5 litres
Sparge – 18 litres

3kg low-colour pale ale malt
1.8kg wheat malt
400g torrified wheat
100g rolled oats
Start of boil 10g any hop with alpha of around 10%
End of boil 200g Hallertauer Hersbrucker, 100g Cluster, 75g Magnum

■ Mash temperature 50°C 20 minutes, stand; 62°C 20 minutes, stand; 65°C 20 minutes, stand; and 68°C 20 minutes, stand.
■ Sparge temperature 75°C, allow 1½ hours for run off. Ensure the spent grain doesn't set like thick porridge by stirring frequently.
■ Boil for 45 minutes as vigorously as possible.
■ Leave hops to stand in the wort for an hour after the heater is off before transferring to fermenting vessel. Fit cover to boiler while you do this. Cool quickly to 25°C as soon as possible after the stand.
■ For fermentation add Wyeast Belgian Wit 3944 or equivalent.
■ Fermentation temp 25°C, ferment for seven days.
■ Condition for seven days at 4°C (or less if possible).
■ Fine and bottle with 1ml fresh yeast and 15g/litre glucose monohydrate in a strong bottle.
■ Condition for a week at 25°C and then cellar for a week.

Chimay

Thwaites

Thornbridge Oatmeal Stout

25 litres
Original gravity 1.050
FG 1.013
ABV 4.9%

Grist
4.59kg pale ale malt
273g chocolate malt
219g crystal malt
109g roasted barley
273g rolled oats
(Assumes 75% efficiency)

Hops
Start of boil 45g East Kent Goldings
End of boil 150g East Kent Goldings and 150g Fuggles

- Mash temperature 66°C.
- Boil 75 minutes as vigorously as possible.
- Leave hops to sit in wort for an hour after heater off before transferring to fermenting vessel. Fit cover to boiler while you do this.
- Leave hops to stand in the wort for an hour after the heater is off before transferring to fermenting vessel. Fit cover to boiler while you do this. Cool quickly to 20°C as soon as possible after the stand.
- For fermentation add Wyeast 1084 or equivalent.
- Fermentation temperature 20°C, ferment for seven days.
- Condition for seven days at 12°C then bottle using half a teaspoon of sugar per 500ml.
- Warm condition for four days at 20°C, then cellar for two weeks to clear.

Frank as Apollo

Winner of Thornbridge/BrewUK home brew competition, created by Paul Carruthers

25 litres
Original gravity 1.046
Final gravity 1.011
Alcohol 4.5%
Total liquor 35.5 litres
Mash liquor 12.5 litres
Bitterness 47 EBU
Colour 19 EBC
Yeast WLP001, US-05 or equivalent

Grist
Pale malt 4.23kg – ratio 85%
Munich malt 495g – ratio 10%
Caramunich 245g – ratio 5%

Hops
Simcoe (aa 12.7%) 13g, add at start of boil, 90 minutes – ratio 10.8%.
Simcoe (aa12.7%) 20g, add 15 minutes from end of boil – ratio 16.2%.
Apollo (aa 19.5%) 20g, add 15 minutes from end of boil – ratio 16.2%.
Apollo (aa 19.5%) 46g, add at end of boil – ratio 37.8%.
Columbus Tomahawk (aa 15%) 23g, add at end of boil – ratio 18.9%.

- Mash at 68°C for 60 minutes.
- Boil for 90 minutes.
- Ferment at 20°C.

SOME HISTORIC BEER RECIPES

With thanks to the Durden Park Beer Circle,
www.durdenparkbeer.org.uk, whose members formed the
club to recreate historic British beers, particularly from around
1840–1914. To brew larger quantities of these beers simply
scale up the ingredients as required.

Simonds' Bitter (1880)

4.5 litres
Original gravity 1.062

1,190g pale malt
226g pale amber malt
22g Fuggles hops
5g Goldings hops in late boil, 2–3g dry hopping

- Mash grain for three hours at 66±1°C. Raise temperature
  to 77°C for 30 minutes.
- Sparge with hot water at 82–85°C to OG or required
  volume.
- Boil with Fuggles hops for 90 minutes and add the
  Goldings hops towards the end of the boil.
- Cool and ferment with a good quality ale yeast.
- Mature three months.

Simonds was a pioneer of pale ale in the 1830s, including
Indian Pale Ale, which the company exported to the British
Army in India. In the 1870s they developed a lighter beer
called 'SB', and in the following decade introduced a new
system known as the 'Burton Union Method'.

William Black's X Ale (1849)

4.5 litres
Original gravity 1.075

1,475g pale malt
32g Goldings Hops

- Mash grain for three hours at 66±1°C. Raise temperature
  to 77°C for 30 minutes.
- Sparge with hot water at 82–85°C to OG or required
  volume.
- Boil with hops for 90 minutes.
- Cool and ferment with a good quality ale yeast.
- Mature for at least six months.

▶ **Hop harvesting is hard physical work that continues whatever
the weather.** (Tim Hampson)

Tim Hampson

Original Porter (circa 1750)

4.5 litres
Original gravity 1.090

1,600g pale malt
226g brown malt
226g crystal malt
112g black malt
42g Fuggles hops

- Using a very stiff mash, mash grain for three hours at 66±1°C. Raise temperature to 77°C for 30 minutes.
- Sparge slowly with hot water at 82–85°C to OG or required volume.
- The first runnings from the sparge are best used for this beer (ie the highest gravity) in order to attain OG 1.090. The further runnings can be used to make a lower gravity beer.
- Boil with hops for 90 minutes.
- Cool and ferment with a good quality ale yeast.
- Mature for at least six months.

In 1750 porters would have contained mostly brown malt, but they cannot be made satisfactorily from present-day brown malts. This recipe is constructed to meet contemporary descriptions of 1750 porter, ie black, strong, bitter and nutritious.

Younger's Export Stout (1897)

A full bodied succulent stout

4.5 litres
Original gravity 1.066–1.068

680g pale malt
454g Carapils malt
70g crystal malt
56g black malt
38g Fuggles or Goldings hops

- Mash grain for three hours at 66±1°C. Raise temperature to 77°C for 30 minutes.
- Sparge with hot water at 82–85°C to OG or required volume.
- Boil with hops for 90 minutes.
- Cool and ferment with a good quality ale yeast.
- Mature six months.

Bottling of high gravity old ales has to be done with care. Priming sugar should be restricted to a quarter or third of normal.

Ushers 60/- Pale Ale (1886)

4.6 litres
Original gravity 1.060

1,135g pale malt
21g hops

- Mash grain for three hours at 66±1°C. Raise temperature to 77°C for 30 minutes.
- Sparge with hot water at 82–85°C to OG or required volume.
- Boil with hops for 90 minutes.
- Cool and ferment with a good quality ale yeast.
- Mature three months.

Whitbread's London Porter (1850)

4.5 litres
Original gravity 1.060

1,020g pale malt
200g brown malt
70g black malt
28g Fuggles or Goldings hops

- Mash grain for three hours at 66±1°C. Raise temperature to 77°C for 30 minutes.
- Sparge with hot water at 82–85°C to OG or required volume.
- Boil with hops for 90 minutes.
- Cool and ferment with a good quality ale yeast.
- Mature four months.

Whitbread's London Porter is one of Durden Park's all-time favourites.

Adding hop flavours to your beer

There's a trend for beers to use pronounced hop flavours. It's very easy to make your own hophead variation on any of the above recipes. Take 25g of hops – American or other New World varieties are often the best for this. The fun is experimenting. Put into a jug and add about 500ml of boiling water. Stir and leave to cool. Strain and add to the beer just before putting it into the barrel or bottle. Or if you don't want to do this you could add some hop oil.

Tim Hampson

APPENDICES
USEFUL BITS

Useful contacts

If you have a problem with your brewing, help is never far away.

A Plus Hops
A supplier of hops
www.aplus-hops.co.uk.

Beer Academy
Provides training courses for amateurs and professionals who wish to increase their understanding and knowledge of beer appreciation.
www.beeracademy.org.

Brewing Network
A US multimedia web resource for home and professional brewers.
www.thebrewingnetwork.com.

Brewlab
A provider of training and analysis services for home and professional brewers, which is based in Sunderland.
www.brewlab.co.uk.

Brew Shop
Excellent supplier of brewing equipment and ingredients, based in Stockport, Cheshire.
www.thebrewshop.com.

Brew UK
Specialist supplier of home brew ingredients and equipment.
www.brewuk.co.uk.

Brupaks
Supplier of raw material and equipment to home and microbrewers.
www.brupaks.com.

Campaign for Real Ale (CAMRA)
Consumer organisation campaigning for cask-conditioned beer and community pubs.
www.camra.org.uk.

Craft Brewing Association
A self-help group of home brewers who wish to improve their beers.
www.craftbrewing.org.uk.

Durden Park Beer Circle
Dedicated to brewing historic British beers, particularly from around 1840–1914.
www.durdenparkbeer.org.uk.

Charles Faram
Hop supplier, stocks more than 100 different varieties of hops.
www.charlesfaram.co.uk.

Home Brew Shop
One of the best-known suppliers of home brew equipment and ingredients.
www.the-home-brew-shop.co.uk.

London Amateur Brewers
An informal group of home brewers from London and the Home Counties who meet to share their skills, knowledge and beer.
http://londonamateurbrewers.wordpress.com.

Malt Miller
Mail order supplier of home brew equipment and ingredients, based in Didcot, Oxfordshire.
www.themaltmiller.co.uk.

Muntons
Supplier of home brewing kits and equipment.
www.muntonshomebrew.com.

National Association of Wine and Beermakers
Organisation that draws together individuals, clubs, and federations in England who are involved in beer and wine making at home. It organises an annual conference and exhibition.
www.nawb.org.uk.

Maltsters' Association
The trade association of the UK malting industry.
www.ukmalt.com.

USA Hops
Site for information on US hop industry.
www.usahops.org.

Glossary

Adjunct – An ingredient other than malted barley used in mashing, such as maize, unmalted barley, rye and wheat.

Aftertaste – The flavour that remains at the back of the mouth and in the throat as the beer is swallowed. It's often different from the first taste.

ABV (alcohol by volume) – A measure of the proportion of alcohol in beer, expressed as a percentage of the overall volume. Most beers are around 5% ABV.

Ale – A word originally used in England to describe an unhopped malt drink. Today it's beer brewed from a top-fermenting yeast with a relatively short, warm fermentation, and it contains hops.

Alpha acid (aa) – One of the natural bittering substances in hops.

Aroma – The smell of beer in the glass.

Attenuation – The degree of conversion of sugar to alcohol and CO2. The higher the attenuation of a beer the dryer it will taste. Sweeter beers are less attenuated.

Barley – The most widely used cereal for conversion into malt for brewing.

Barley wine – A strong fruity beer that's often more than 8% ABV. Reputedly its name is said to come from the time of the Napoleonic Wars, when Britons were encouraged to drink beer rather than French wine.

Barrel – A container for holding liquid. In the UK a 36-gallon barrel is also used as a unit of measurement to gauge large volumes of beer.

Beer – The generic term for cereal-based fermented brews, including ale, lager, stout and porter. Around the world, it is known by the following names:
— *Alus*: Latvian, Lithuanian
— *Beer*: Thai
— *Beerah:* Arabic
— *Beoir*: Irish
— *Bere*: Romanian
— *Bia*: Swahili
— *Bier*: Afrikaans, Breton, Dutch, German
— *Bière*: French
— *Bierke*: Flemish
— *Biertje*: Dutch
— *Bir*: Indonesian, Malay
— *Bira*: Greek, Turkish
— *Birra*: Italian
— *Birrë*: Albanian
— *Bi-ru*: Japanese
— *Biyar*: Hindi
— *Bjór*: Icelandic
— *Cerveja*: Portuguese
— *Cervesa*: Catalan
— *Cerveza*: Spanish
— *Cwrw*: Welsh
— *Garagardo*: Basque
— *Øl*: Danish, Norwegian
— *Öl*: Swedish
— *Õlu*: Estonian
— *Olut*: Finnish
— *Píji*: Chinese (Mandarin)
— *Pivo*: Bosnian, Croatian, Czech, Macedonian, Russian, Serbian, Slovak, Slovene, Ukrainian and other Slavonic languages
— *Piwo*: Polish
— *Sharaab*: Urdu
— *Sör*: Hungarian

Beer engine – A suction pump, used to draw beer out of a cask. Often known as a handpull or handpump.

Best bitter – A self-selecting term for which there's no precise definition. Traditionally a brewer uses the term to describe a beer that has a higher alcohol content than his standard bitter. Frequently the strength will be between 4.0 and 4.6% ABV.

Bitter – A copper-coloured ale which is usually well hopped. It was once the most popular beer in Britain. Generally a standard or ordinary bitter's strength will be between 3.3 and 4.0% ABV; best bitter's generally between 4.0 and 4.6%; and special or strong bitters 4.7% or more.

Bitterness – Beer's bitterness is derived from the hops used in its manufacture. Beer bitterness is expressed in International Bitterness Units (IBUs), which represent a measurement of the intensity of the beer's bitterness. A lightly hopped US-style lager can have a bitterness reading as low as five IBUs. A highly hopped American-style IPA can have 70 IBUs or even more. In the UK most ales range in bitterness from about 16 to 50 IBUs. Beers brewed with a high proportion of malt can have the same level of bitterness as a weaker brew, but won't taste so bitter because of the sweetness of the sugars from the malt.

Body – The fullness of flavour that malt creates in a beer.

Bottle-conditioned – A beer that's bottled with some yeast. The beer will continue to mature and its condition will change while in the bottle. Depending on the beer it may have to be poured carefully to avoid the yeast clouding the beer in the glass.

Cath Harries

Bottom-fermentation – The Continental European method of fermenting wort, used mainly for lager brewing. A yeast that sinks to the bottom of the beer is used, instead of the kind used to ferment ale, which rises to the top.

Brewery conditioned – A beer that's been filtered and sometimes pasteurised in the brewery instead of being allowed to continue to ferment, or condition, in the cask or bottle.

Brewpub – A pub where beer is brewed on the premises.

Bright beer – Beer that's been chilled and filtered to take out the yeast.

Brown ale – Beer brewed from darker malts, usually bottled and often low in alcohol content.

Bulk barrel – A beer measurement unit of 36 gallons, irrespective of the size of the containers in which the beer is contained. A bulk barrel is equivalent to a metric measure of 1.64 hectolitres.

Burtonisation – The treatment of water with gypsum and other minerals to make it similar to the hard water drawn from wells in the Burton upon Trent area.

Burton union – A system of fermenting wort once common in Burton upon Trent but now used only by Marston's. The wort is fermented in a series of large casks and excess yeast is gathered in a trough that runs along the top.

CAMRA (Campaign for Real Ale) – A British consumer movement, founded in 1971 with the aim of preserving and promoting naturally conditioned ale and the places – mainly pubs and clubs – where it's served.

Caramel – A form of burnt sugar used to add colour to beer.

Carbonation – The process of injecting carbon dioxide into beer to replace the natural carbon dioxide lost when the beer is filtered or pasteurised or both.

Cask – A container, usually made from steel or aluminium though sometimes of plastic, in which beer undergoes a secondary fermentation. It has two openings, one to allow the beer out, the other to allow carbon dioxide to escape as the beer matures.

Cask breather – A system that adds carbon dioxide to a cask as the beer is drawn out. It prevents air – the enemy of beer – coming in contact with the beer.

Cask-conditioned – A beer packaged in a cask or bottle without the presence of added carbon dioxide, which is allowed to undergo secondary fermentation.

Cask Marque – A scheme run by an independent non-profit-making body called the Cask Marque Trust, which awards certificates and plaques to pubs whose cask beer reaches set standards.

Chilled and filtered – A beer that's had solid particles such as yeast removed by being chilled so that the particles sink to the bottom. It is then filtered.

Chocolate malt – Dark malt that's roasted after being kilned; used for flavour and colour in porter, stout and other dark beers.

Cold break – Precipitate of hop residue and protein that coagulates when wort is cooled after boiling.

Cold liquor tank – A container in a brewery used to hold water before it's heated for mashing. The water used for brewing in a brewery is always called liquor.

Tim Hampson

Collar – The frothy, bubbly head on top of a glass of beer.

Colour – Three methods are commonly used to measure the colour of beer: EBC (European Brewery Convention), Lovibond (devised by Joseph Williams Lovibond, a British brewer), and SRM (standard reference method). EBC grades beers upwards from light to dark, so that pale lager may measure four degrees on its scale and Imperial stout 138. Lovibond and SRM range from two degrees for pale lager to 70 for Imperial stout, though not many beers other than stouts and porters are above 30 degrees.

Condition – Most beer should have a natural sparkle, derived from the carbon dioxide dissolved in it. A beer in good condition will release a cloudy bubble of carbon dioxide as it's poured.

Conditioning – The process of allowing beer to continue to ferment after being taken out of the fermenting vessel. Beer is conditioned in tanks at the brewery, in casks in the pub cellar or in bottles.

Cooling jacket – A cover for a cask, with cold water running through it to keep the beer cool.

Copper – A large container normally made of stainless steel but which was once made from copper, where wort is boiled with hops. It's often called a kettle.

Crown cap or crown cork – A metal disc crimped on to the top of a bottle; the most common means of sealing beer bottles.

Crystal malt – Pale brown malt, rich in natural sugars.

Diacetyl – A buttery, butterscotch flavour that's a natural by-product of fermentation and occurs is many beers. A small amount of diacetyl is considered appropriate for some ale styles, such as an American Amber, but it's normally regarded as a no-no in lagers. Usually lagers are kept cold throughout the fermentation process. However, if you warm up the beer towards the end of secondary fermentation (typically up to 16°C) the diacetyl level will drop pretty fast. You should leave it for two days – this is known as the 'diacetyl rest' – before dropping the temperature back down again.

Dimethyl sulphide (DMS) – A sulphur compound beneficial to the taste and bouquet of lager at concentrations below 0.1ppm. At higher concentrations it imparts a bouquet often described as 'cooked-vegetable' or 'sweet-corn'.

Draught – A beer that's poured into a glass from a tap or pump.

Dray – A brewery vehicle for delivering beer. Traditionally they were horse-drawn, but today they're motorised.

Dregs – The solids in an unfiltered beer after it's been run into casks or bottles. The dregs are made of yeast and, in dry-hopped beers, small pieces of hop cones.

Drop bright – Cask beer is said to have 'dropped bright' when it's cleared and the sediment has completely settled below the level of the tap.

Dry-hopping – The practice of putting a quantity of fragrant hops directly into a full cask of beer to improve its aroma.

Esters – Organic compounds formed by the reaction of alcohols and acids during brewing. There are more than 80 of them and they give beer fruity flavours and aromas.

Ethanol – The type of alcohol in beer, formed by yeast from malt sugars.

Fermentation – The process of converting sweet wort into beer by allowing yeast to feed off the sugars, creating carbon dioxide and alcohol.

Fermenting vessel – A tank where sweet wort is fermented into beer.

FG – Final gravity. When the specific gravity is measured at the end of fermentation it is known as the final gravity. The FG shows how much sugar is left in the beer.

Filtration – Removal of solid particles from beer by passing it through a porous substance such as kieselguhr or a centrifuge.

Final gravity – A measure of a beer's density after fermentation compared to that of water. The lower the final gravity, compared with original gravity, the higher the alcohol content.

Fined – A beer that's been clarified by the addition of finings.

Finings – A substance added to cask-conditioned beer that attracts the floaty bits, mainly yeast, which then sink to the bottom leaving the beer clear. Finings are traditionally made from isinglass, a natural form of collagen, which is derived from the swim bladders of sturgeon.

Finish – An alternative word for aftertaste, the flavour that remains at the back of the mouth and in the throat after swallowing beer.

Gambrinus – A patron saint of beer.

Golden ale – A new style of pale, well-hopped and quenching beer that developed in the 1980s as brewers attempted to win younger drinkers from heavily-promoted lager brands.

Green – A beer that isn't yet properly matured or is made using freshly picked hops.

Grist – Malt grains that have been ground into a coarse flour by milling, prior to mashing.

Gruit – A mixture of herbs and spices used to flavour beer in the medieval period. It could include such things as henbane, wild rosemary, heather, ginger, spruce, juniper and bog myrtle.

Handpump or handpull – A suction pump also known as a beer engine, consisting of a tall handle on a bar top, connected to a piston inside a cylinder, used for raising beer from cellar to glass.

Head – The frothy collar on top of beer. It mainly consists of carbon dioxide in bubbles surrounded by protein.

Hop – A perennial climbing plant that's grown for its small cones (or flowers), which are known as hops. Hops provide beer with its bitter flavour and aroma. They also help clear the beer and protect it against unwanted bacteria.

Hop back – Equipment used to strain wort through the used hops after boiling in a copper.

Hop extract – A preparation of hops used instead of whole hops or hop pellets.

Hop garden – A farm where hops are grown in Kent and other counties of the South of England.

Hop pellets – Dried, powdered and compressed hops, which help save space.

Tim Hampson

Tim Hampson

Hop pocket – A large sack containing hops.

Hop yard – A farm where hops are grown in Herefordshire and Worcestershire.

Hot break – Flocculent precipitate of insoluble proteins that forms during the boiling of hopped beer wort.

Hot liquor tank – A container used to hold water after it's been heated for mashing.

IBU – International bitter unit. See *Bitterness*.

IPA or India Pale Ale – The beer that changed the face of brewing early in the 19th century. The new technologies of the industrial revolution enabled brewers to use pale malts to fashion beers that were genuinely golden or pale bronze in colour. First brewed in London and Burton upon Trent, IPAs were strong in alcohol and high in hops. The preservative character of the hops helped keep the beers in good condition during long sea journeys. Beers with less alcohol and hops developed for the domestic market were known simply as pale ale.

Isinglass – A natural protein derived from the swim bladders of fish, traditionally sturgeon, which is used to clarify beer.

Keg – A sealed cylindrical container for pasteurised and pressurised beer. It has only one opening, to let the beer out, unlike a cask, which has a second opening to vent the beer.

Keg beer – Beer that's usually been filtered, pasteurised and pressurised with carbon dioxide, nitrogen or a mixture of both. It's stored in kegs and doesn't mature in the pub cellar.

Kettle – An alternative name for a copper.

Keystone – A small circular bung, made of wood or plastic, placed in the hole on one of the flat ends of a cask. A tap is inserted through the keystone to allow the beer out.

Kieselguhr – A form of soft, fine-grained diatomaceous earth, used in the filtration of beer.

Krausening – Adding a small amount of freshly brewed beer to one undergoing lengthy maturation. It triggers a new flurry of fermentation and natural carbonation.

Lactose – A form of sugar that was traditionally extracted from whey, the liquid remaining after milk has been curdled and strained, though these days it isn't likely to be milk-derived. Lactose is used in brewing to provide the sweetness in cream stout or milk stout (such as Mackeson).

Lager – In the UK lager is usually a light-coloured, golden yellow beer that's served chilled at 8°C or even lower. It owes its origins to beers from Continental Europe produced by bottom fermentation at low temperatures and held in store (*lager* in German) for long periods.

Lauter tun – A vessel for separating the wort from the solid components of the mash. After mashing the brewer needs to separate the syrupy sweet wort from the spent grain. The oldest and the most widely used piece of equipment to do this is the lauter tun, essentially a large sieve.

Light ale – The name used by some brewers for bottled pale ale.

Lightstruck – Beer can become lightstruck or sunstruck if it comes in contact with ultraviolet light or sunlight. The light can quickly change a component in the hop content of the beer into a nauseous, sulphur-smelling component that's often described as 'skunky'. For this reason most brewers prefer to put beer into brown bottles, which ultraviolet light can't penetrate, rather than clear glass.

Cath Harries

Lines – The pipes leading from casks and kegs in the pub cellar to the pumps and taps on the bar.

Liquor – The brewers' term for water.

Maize – A cereal that's high in starch and is sometimes used as an adjunct.

Malt – Barley grains that have been allowed to germinate after being steeped in water and then heated in a kiln, to stop the germination at a point where the grains are ideal for brewing and their sugars can be released in the mash tun.

Malt extract – A preparation of sugars extracted from malt and normally concentrated into a syrup. Used by some brewers instead of whole grains.

Maltings – The place where barley is converted into malt.

Malt mill – A machine that grinds open malt grains into a grist ready for mashing.

Maltster – The person who operates a maltings.

Mashing – The process of extracting natural sugars from malt by mixing it with hot water.

Tim Hampson

Mash tun – The vessel in which malt is mixed, or mashed, with hot water.

Mild – A lightly hopped beer, usually below 3.5% ABV but increasingly being brewed stronger. Mild is one of the most traditional of British beer styles. Usually dark brown in colour, due to the use of well-roasted malts or barley – though lighter versions are also produced – it's less hopped than bitters and often has a chocolate character with nutty and burnt flavours.

Milling – The process of cracking open and grinding malt grains into a grist ready for mashing.

Mixed gas – A mixture usually of carbon dioxide and nitrogen used to carbonate beer. Guinness was among the first beers to be packaged in kegs with mixed gas. Nitrokeg beers, which became popular in the 1990s, are filtered and sometimes pasteurised ales stored and served with mixed gas.

Naturally conditioned – Description of beer that continues to ferment and mature in a cask or bottle.

Ninkasi – Ancient Sumerian goddess of beer. Sumer was in Mesopotamia, now a part of Iran. The 4,000-year-old poem *A Hymn to Ninkasi* contains a recipe for beer.

Nitrogen – A gaseous element, forming almost 80% of air, used in combination with carbon dioxide as a mixed gas to pressurise some beers.

Nitrokeg – Beers that are filtered and often pasteurised before being pressurised in kegs with a mixture of nitrogen and carbon dioxide.

Oast house – A building where hops are dried after being harvested.

Old ale – A beer that's been allowed to mature for several months, or in some cases much longer. The style is often associated with darker, stronger beers.

Original gravity (OG) – A measure of the fermentable and unfermentable material in the wort before fermentation. OG gives the brewer an idea of the potential alcoholic strength of the beer. Beer with an OG of 1.050 has 50 parts of solid material, by weight, to every 1,000 parts of water. As a rule of thumb a beer with an OG of 1.050 is likely to produce a 5% ABV beer, while an OG of 1.040 would produce a 4% brew.

Oxidation – Beer can oxidise when it comes in contact with air, which can result in a chemical reaction that produces some unpleasant flavours and aromas.

Pale ale – Beer brewed from lightly kilned pale malt, usually of medium strength, available on draught or in bottles.

Paraflow – A cooler used to lower the temperature of wort as it's moved from the copper to the fermenting vessel.

Pasteurisation – Sterilising beer by heating it to kill off microorganisms and to stop fermentation.

PET – Polyethylene terephthalate, a plastic material often used to make bottles.

pH – A scale (1–14) that measures the degree of acidity or alkalinity of a solution, in which a value of 7 represents neutrality. A value of 1 is most acidic, a value of 14 is most alkaline.

Pils, Pilsener, Pilsner – A style of pale, golden, fragrant beer originating in Plzen or Pilsen in Bohemia, now part of the Czech Republic, where a beer was first produced by bottom-fermentation in 1842. Worldwide the name has become a generic term to describe many pale-coloured beers that have no connection with the original Pilsner.

Pitching – Adding yeast to wort.

Polypin – A polythene container, usually inside a cardboard box, containing 4½ gallons of beer.

Porter – An English dark beer, first brewed in the 18th century. Stout began as a strong (or 'stout') version of porter.

Priming – The addition of a fermentable material, usually sugar, to beer during conditioning to create a sparkle during secondary fermentation.

Racking – Filling casks with beer.

Real ale – Another name for cask-conditioned beer.

Rice – A cereal used for its starch content by some brewers, usually as an adjunct.

Runnings – After a mash is finished, the liquid drawn through the mash bed is known as 'runnings'.

Saccharomyces – A genus of fungus that includes many species of yeast. *Saccharomyces cerevisiae* is used to ferment ale and *Saccharomyces cerevisiae*, now usually called *Saccharomyces eubayanus*, is used in lager.

Sample room – The place where you'll often find the brewer; it's an area in a brewery where the quality of the beer can be monitored.

Secondary fermentation – The process of beer continuing to ferment and mature in a conditioning tank in the brewery or in a cask or bottle.

Sediment – The deposit, consisting mainly of yeast, which sinks to the bottom of a cask of beer in a pub cellar.

Shive – Wooden or plastic bung with penetrable core that allows carbon dioxide to escape from a cask, controlled by a peg called a spile.

Skimming – Removing the yeast from the top of fermenting beer.

Sparging – Spraying hot water over malt in a mash tun to maximise the release of sweet fermentable material.

Spent hops – Hops left in the copper after the wort has been boiled.

Spent malt – Grains of malted barley left in the mash tun after the wort has been run off.

Spile – Wooden or plastic peg knocked into the centre of a shive to control the rate of carbon dioxide escaping from a cask. Soft spiles are porous and allow gas to escape relatively quickly; hard spiles retain the carbon dioxide.

Strength – The strength of beer is usually expressed as its alcohol by volume, or ABV. See *Original Gravity (OG)*.

Cath Harries

Top-fermentation – A method of fermenting wort in which the yeast rises to the top of the beer. This process is used when brewing ale.

Trub – The sediment at the bottom of the fermenter consisting of hot and cold break material, hop bits, and dead yeast.

Underback – A vessel underneath a mash tun where wort is collected after mashing.

Wheat – A cereal, malted or unmalted, used in brewing alongside malted barley, either to stabilise the beer or to produce wheat beer. It also helps to produce the head on a beer.

Whirlpool – Commercially, brewers of hoppy beers will often whirlpool their beers post boil, after the addition of the final hops and before cooling. Creating a gentle whirlpool effect, either with a pump, or by hand using a large spoon or stirrer, settles the trub into a nice cone in the centre of the kettle, allowing the rest of the clearer wort to be drawn off into the fermenter. While it is important to chill the hot wort quickly, a home brewer could allow the still hot wort to steep for 10 minutes.

Wort – Unfermented beer, the solution of sugars, dextrins and flavourings prior to fermentation.

Yeast – A fungus used during fermentation, which as part of its lifecycle transforms wort into beer by converting the soluble sugars from malt into alcohol and carbon dioxide.

Zymurgy – The science of brewing and fermentation.

Cath Harries